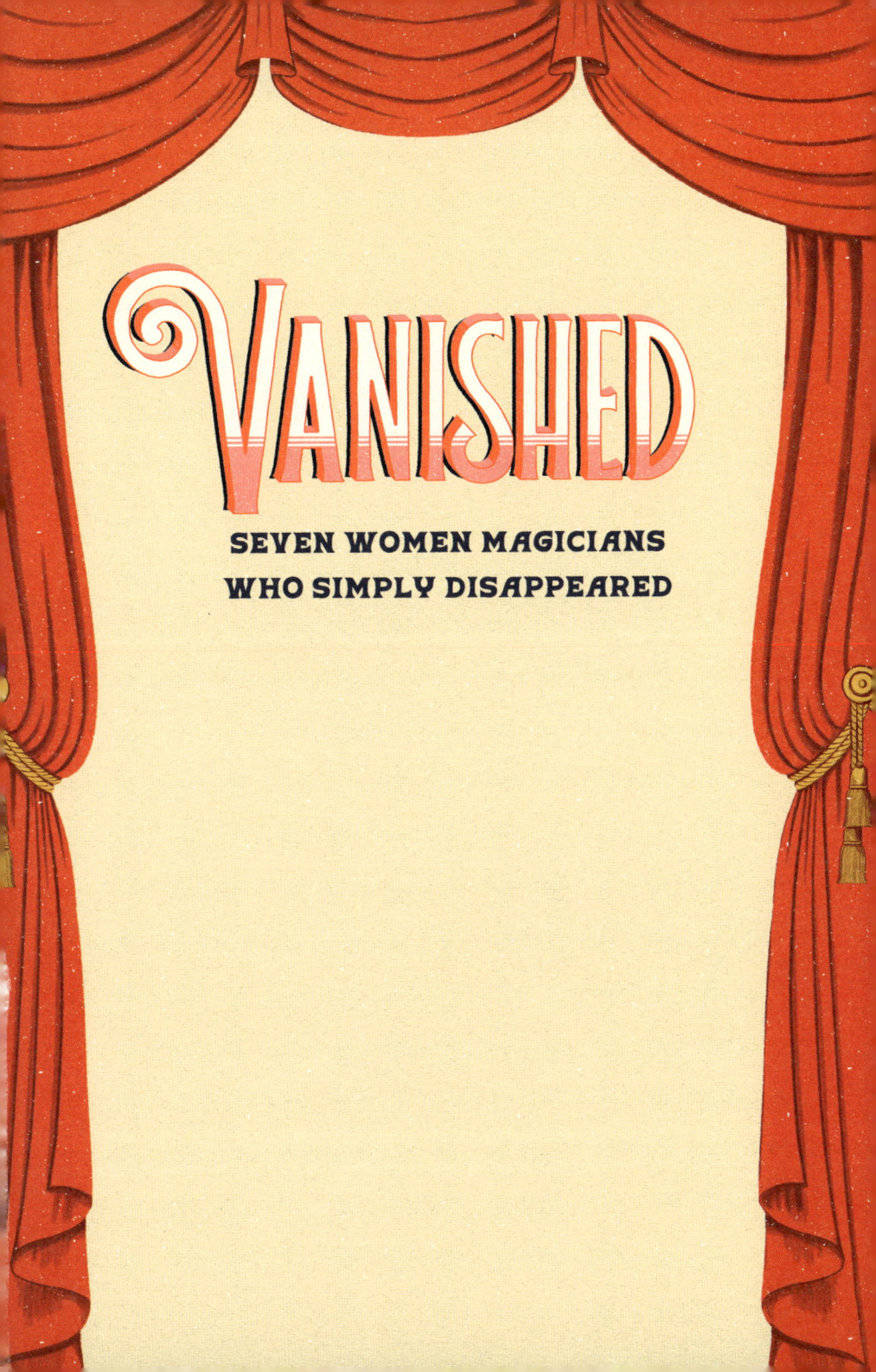

VANISHED

SEVEN WOMEN MAGICIANS WHO SIMPLY DISAPPEARED

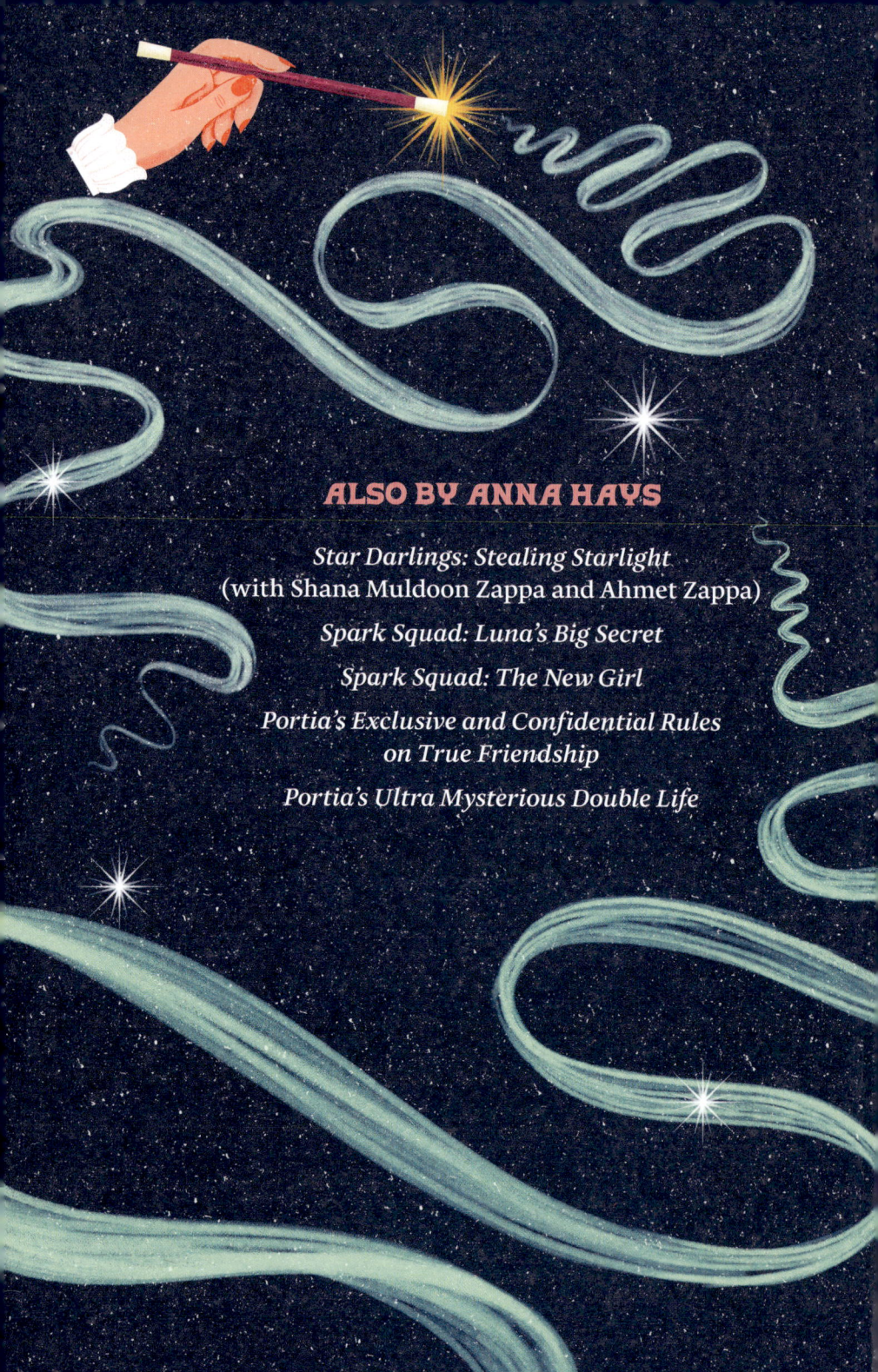

ALSO BY ANNA HAYS

Star Darlings: Stealing Starlight
(with Shana Muldoon Zappa and Ahmet Zappa)

Spark Squad: Luna's Big Secret

Spark Squad: The New Girl

*Portia's Exclusive and Confidential Rules
on True Friendship*

Portia's Ultra Mysterious Double Life

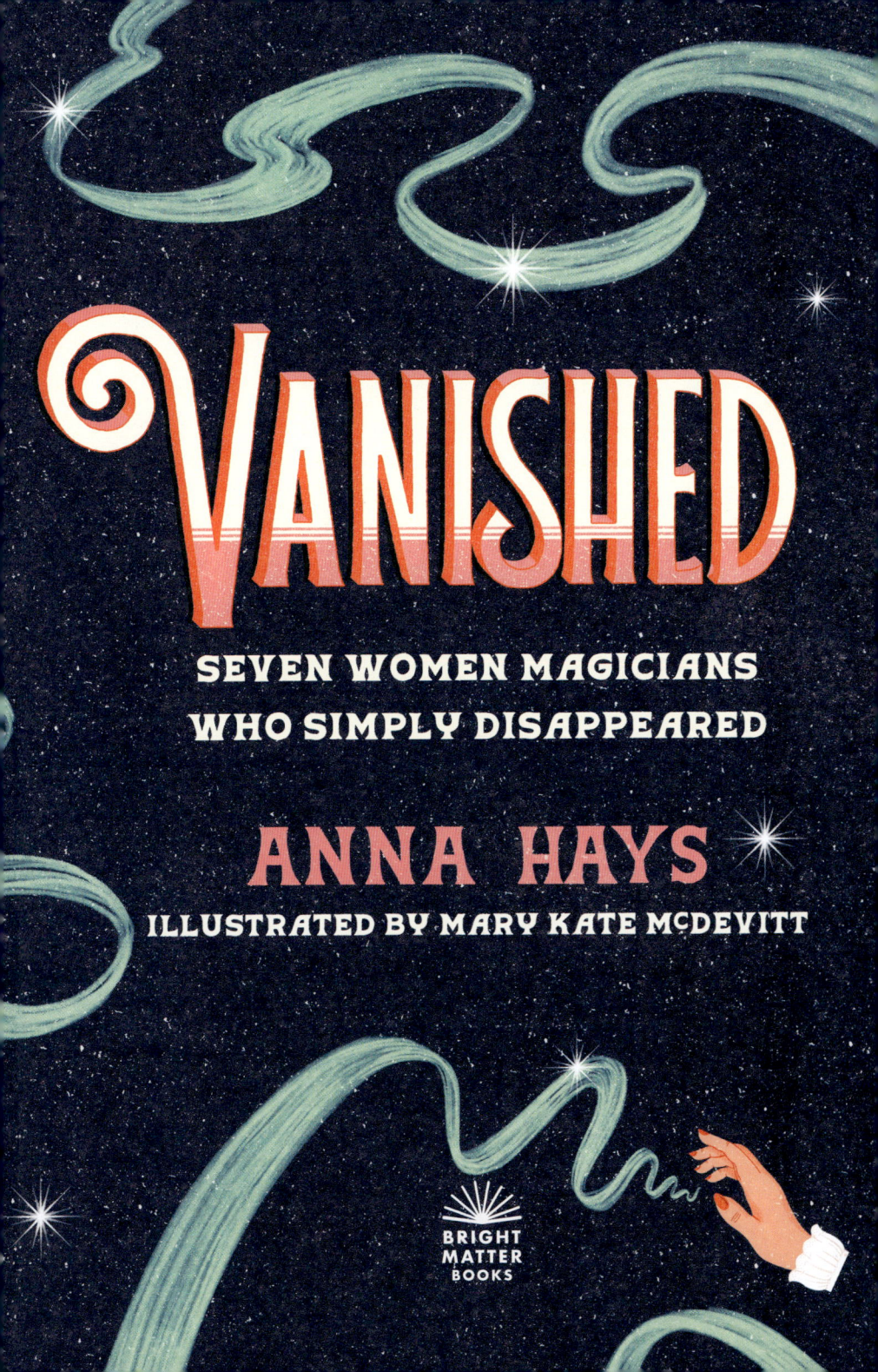

Vanished

SEVEN WOMEN MAGICIANS WHO SIMPLY DISAPPEARED

ANNA HAYS

ILLUSTRATED BY MARY KATE McDEVITT

BRIGHT
MATTER
BOOKS

Library of Congress Cataloging-in-Publication Data is available upon request.
ISBN 978-0-593-71255-9 (trade)—ISBN 978-0-593-71256-6 (lib. bdg.)—
ISBN 978-0-593-80543-5 (ebook)

The text of this book is set in 10.85-point Eloquence.
Interior design by Jen Valero

MANUFACTURED IN CHINA
10 9 8 7 6 5 4 3 2 1
First Edition

The authorized representative in the EU for product safety and compliance is
Penguin Random House Ireland, Morrison Chambers, 32 Nassau Street, Dublin
D02 YH68, Ireland, https://eu-contact.penguin.ie.

TO BUZZ, BEN, WILL, AND WILLOW

CONTENTS

INTRODUCTION

After I met my husband, Buzz—who is a magician member of The Magic Castle, a popular magic club in Hollywood—I was suddenly immersed in the world of magic, meeting a wide variety of conjurers. I quickly noticed how few women were performing and became curious about the role of women in magic history. I had a hunch that there was at least one incredible story waiting to be unearthed, and I wanted to tell it! I started searching. Then I found her, or maybe she found me? Her name was Anna Eva Fay, and she was one of the most famous mediums and mind readers of the Victorian era. As I dug deeper, I discovered that there were others like her, women magicians who had achieved great heights, who were once world-renowned but have since vanished from history.

Inspired, I continued my research, which was more like an excavation than a visit to the library. After scouring newspaper clippings, advertisements, notices, and reviews, I realized that trying to create portraits of these forgotten women magicians would not be easy. I would have to become a detective to piece together their stories from fragments of their past, like scattered clues in a cold case. During my journey, I talked with magicians and collectors about this crucial and missing piece of history. They assured me that I was on to something. I kept digging.

Then a bit of magic happened. While researching, I was lucky enough to meet the legendary magician David Copperfield, who invited me to his private museum and library in Las Vegas, the International Museum and Library of the Conjuring Arts. He instructed me and my family, along with a small group of other invited guests, to meet him at midnight at a secret location. For the next three hours, he led us through his priceless collection of magic artifacts, posters, and props that date back hundreds of years. At one point, he showed us an area that he was still developing, a section dedicated solely to women magicians. There were photographs, costumes, and props on display, featuring some of the women I had discovered in my search.

After the tour, David invited me to return to his library to do more research. With the help of his archivist, Glenda, I spent hours poring through articles, images, scrapbooks, and clippings. With each new detail I uncovered from this treasure trove of sources, I was convinced that these women's stories were a rich and untapped chapter in history.

I had found my story! Well, more like *stories*. From the amazing women I had discovered, I chose seven to explore in *Vanished*. Each represents a unique contribution to magic. Although on the surface they led very different lives, they all found their calling at a young age and worked tirelessly to perfect their craft, navigating careers for which there was no precedent. These trailblazers were complex and gifted magicians who forged their own destinies, reflecting the true American spirit: independent, resilient, and bold. But there was a twist. Their successes were based on illusions, tricks, and deceptions, which only added to the intrigue and mystery of their remarkable lives. Bringing these women magicians back into the spotlight would be the ultimate magic trick—the big finale!

My hope with *Vanished* is that when you read these incredible true tales of fearless women, you too will brave the impossible and live a life of passion and adventure.

ANNA EVA FAY

PHANTOM PRINCESS

THE MEDIUM

MARCH 31, 1851–MAY 12, 1927

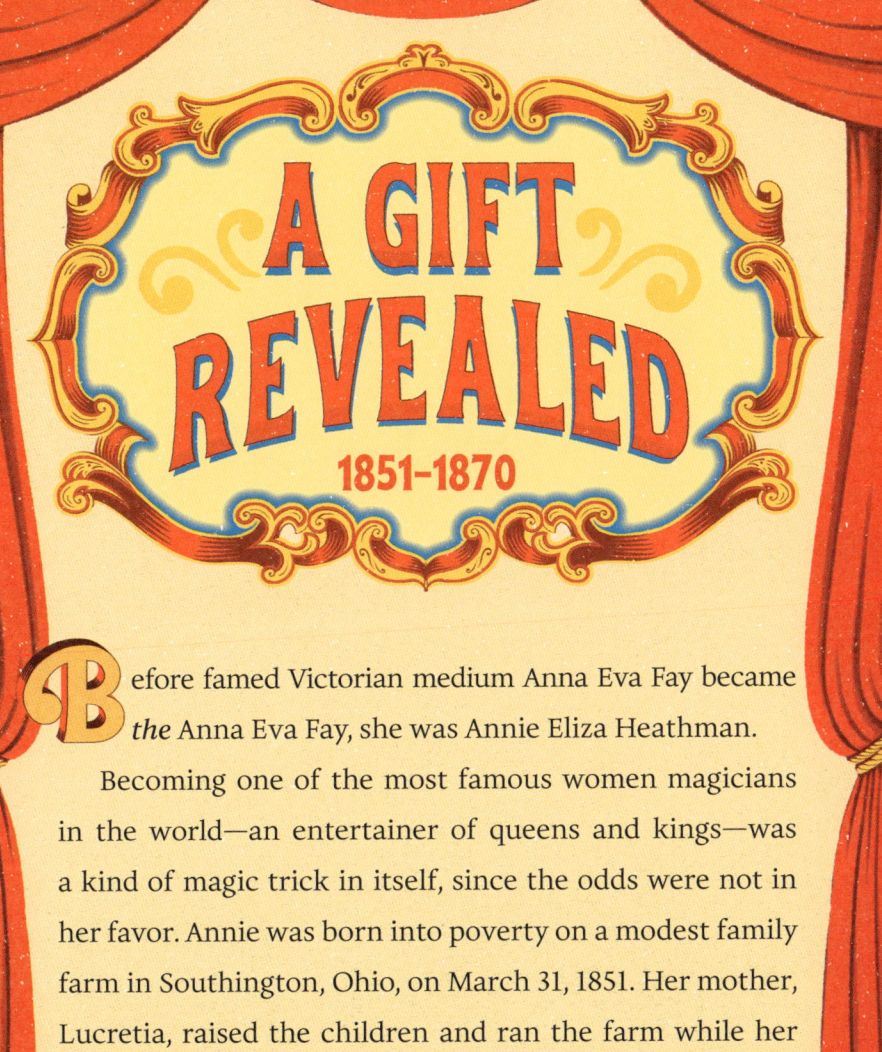

A GIFT REVEALED

1851–1870

Before famed Victorian medium Anna Eva Fay became *the* Anna Eva Fay, she was Annie Eliza Heathman. Becoming one of the most famous women magicians in the world—an entertainer of queens and kings—was a kind of magic trick in itself, since the odds were not in her favor. Annie was born into poverty on a modest family farm in Southington, Ohio, on March 31, 1851. Her mother, Lucretia, raised the children and ran the farm while her father, Joel, worked as a shoemaker. He sold handmade leather shoes door to door and often traveled far into the countryside, not returning until dark. As the oldest child,

Annie took on household duties to help her mother. She would have planted and harvested the backyard garden, canned and pickled the produce for winter, washed and hung out the family clothes, and cared for her younger siblings. Lucretia taught Annie at a young age what it took to survive. Annie loved and admired her mother and found comfort in her strength and resilience. Her life as a young girl appeared simple, unaffected by the world's troubles, though a Civil War had been declared and the country was fiercely divided.

Then, in a single moment, everything changed. In 1862, when Annie was just eleven years old, her mother died suddenly from complications of giving birth to Annie's sister Eunice. The tragedy haunted Annie for the rest of her life, but it also transformed her. Since her father couldn't support and care for his children on his own, he sent all but his infant daughter to surrounding farms as foster children. At the time, farmers willingly took in children to work in the fields. Most of the children who provided extra hands for their foster families were obedient and toiled away without complaining. But Annie refused to accept her fate. She was lonely and restless, and longed to return to her family farm. Each night, after performing domestic tasks that included sweeping the wooden floorboards, tending the hearth, and toiling the land for a family of strangers, she plotted her big escape.

One night, while her foster family slept, Annie slipped

out into the darkness. In the cold night air, she ran as fast as she could toward her family home. The next morning, a neighbor discovered her asleep on the side of the road. Annie's escape had failed. And worse, it had angered her father. She pleaded to stay with him, promising to take care of her baby sister and help run the farm. He refused to take her back. He couldn't afford to support another child. Now her future was more uncertain since she had not behaved as was expected of a foster child. More discouraging, her father placed her with another foster family within days of her escape attempt, this time farther away from the farm. Annie felt helpless and alone.

Annie didn't know it then, but her new foster family set her on a path that would change her life forever. Almon Bruce (A. B.) French, her foster father, was a respected medium in the Spiritualist community in northern Ohio. Spiritualists believed that people known as mediums could contact spirits from the great beyond and communicate with the dead. A. B. French gave religious lectures, published writings in Spiritualist journals, and performed séances in neighboring farms and homesteads. Followers of Spiritualism met in small circles around the country, promoting the idea of life after death and the existence of a soul. During this time, mediums used their skills to create the illusion of receiving messages from the spirit world. Even if they weren't really communicating with the dead, they still

provided much needed comfort to those in mourning.

As a boy, A. B. French claimed that a spirit appeared and spoke to him. He believed that he possessed a special power—he could speak to ghosts. His mother, also a medium, claimed that she too could speak to the dead. She began to train Almon in the art of contacting spirits and delivering their messages to loved ones. Together, they traveled throughout the Midwest conducting sé-ances and "raising spirits from the grave."

When Annie arrived at the French family's doorstep, the Spiritualist movement was gaining popularity in America. By some accounts, there were over 10 million Spiritualists around the time of the Civil War. At first, A.B. put Annie to work performing domestic chores. But eventually he needed another hand at the séance table. His children were younger than Annie, and they didn't show an interest or talent for conjuring, which means performing an illusion. He decided to teach Annie the skills of the art of mediumship. She took to it quickly and showed great promise. Encouraged, French began teaching her more skills. She learned how to fix her eyes on the person across the table and ask simple questions: "What brings you here?" "Are you in search of some-thing?" "Is someone in your family ill?" "Have you lost a loved one?" French showed Annie how to search for clues as they answered. A clue might have been an eye twitch, a turn of the head, or a deep sigh. These silent responses are called tells. A tell reveals what a person is thinking without them saying a word.

From these movements and sounds, Annie learned to interpret the sitter's emotional weaknesses. She showed a natural instinct for picking up the signs and enchanted even the most skeptical guests at the table with her insights. It's possible that by acting as a messenger from the great beyond, Annie felt closer to her own lost mother. A fire lit inside of her. She had found a talent that inspired her. Little Annie Heathman had a hunch that pretending to conjure the dead was the key to her escape to a better life.

After only a few months of training, French recognized Annie's eagerness and natural abilities at the séance table. She could be valuable to him by attracting sitters. More séances meant more income in the home. He continued to mentor her, sharing his magic secrets. Annie soon mastered the deceptive art of table tilting. Tilting or raising tables created the illusion of a spirit's presence. It was achieved in a few ways. French might have shown Annie how to place a hidden knife or fork under the table so that she could raise the table undetected. Or there could have been a hook attached to Annie's belt or tucked inside her long sleeve to tilt the table. French also taught her that a medium needed

PHANTOM PRINCESS

to research before each séance. That meant talking to neighbors and family members of those who sought messages from lost loved ones or visiting graveyards in nearby towns to learn the names of those who had passed on. Annie diligently followed her foster father's instructions, developing the skills she needed to perform convincingly during the séances.

Although described as frail and soft-spoken, Annie knew how to draw sitters into the séance with her intensity. French soon taught her even more tricks to add to her repertoire, like how to rap out the alphabet by shaking the floorboards with her toes, one rap at a time. She learned to spell out each letter with a tap of her toe until she revealed a message from a visiting spirit. Annie also performed automatic writing, where she acted as if she were transcribing a message from a spirit using a pencil and paper. She thrived with each challenge, relishing the spotlight.

Annie spent the next seven years conducting séances. She traveled from farm to farm and table to table, conjuring spirits by candlelight for families who longed to connect with a loved one. She developed finely tuned skills and great confidence as a medium during those teenage years. In 1869, when Annie turned eighteen, it was time for her to step out on her own. Only bits and pieces of her life during this period are known. It appears that she attempted to return to Southington and reunite with her father, hoping he'd accept her back into the family home. When Annie arrived, she discovered that he had since remarried, and she had a new half sister named Delilah. She also quickly realized that her stepmother, Eliza Kibler, wanted nothing to do with her. Her father, once again, coldheartedly sent her on her way.

Despite the setback, Annie persevered. She now possessed a skill that could earn her an income, a unique position for a young woman at the time. And for the rest of the country, Spiritualism was no longer simply a curiosity or a phase. It had evolved into a popular movement with its own leadership, philosophy, and newspapers. The rise of this new religion coincided with a fragile country wearily emerging from the Civil War. More than 600,000 lives had been lost. Diseases such as yellow fever, smallpox, and typhus threatened, and there were still no cures. A cloud of fear covered the country. Mediums were thought to have the power to reconnect families with their loved ones, at a time when many families were grieving. Annie's spirit-conjuring skills were about to pay off.

She began her independent life as a working medium with a new name. Since Eliza was the name of Annie's callous stepmother, Annie changed her middle name from Eliza to Eva. Annie Eva Heathman stepped into the spotlight, no longer under the shadow of A. B. French or anyone else. She conducted séances in a small rented schoolhouse in a town near her father's home. Soon local Spiritualist leaders took notice of her exceptional gift. Word spread. Spiritualist newspapers called Annie the new wonder. Her talent for table tilting and rapping out messages, combined with her ability to convince audiences that her visions were authentic, created a sensation. As her reputation grew, so did her ambition. Annie knew that there was more for her to achieve outside the small Spiritualist circles of rural Ohio.

In 1871, Annie was introduced to a medium ten years her senior named Henry Melville Fay. She had never met anyone quite like him. A far cry from her distant father and stern foster father, Henry impressed her with his lively talk of touring the country conjuring spirits for profit and traveling across the ocean to Europe with his bag of tricks. His showbiz experience, charismatic personality, and, most of all, business savvy caught her attention. She was smitten. Henry took an immediate interest in Annie too. It was as if a door had suddenly opened. Like a magic trick, Annie's life beyond performing countryside séances was revealed to her. Even though Victorian-era American women couldn't vote or hold powerful positions, female mediums could find their roles in society onstage reading minds and conjuring spirits.

Henry knew he had struck gold when he met Annie. The truth was that he had returned to his family home in Akron, Ohio, to escape a growing number of people who doubted his act and wanted to expose him. Exposure is the act of a skeptic publicly displaying how a trick is performed before an audience, with the goal of unveiling the trickery behind the mediums who claimed to awaken the dead. Exposures were performed live or published in popular newspapers and Spiritualist newsletters. They had become commonplace since mediums had started charging money for ticketed public performances. Henry wanted to reinvent himself before returning to the touring circuit. His career needed a boost and a new attraction. He saw Annie as the perfect antidote to the doubters who had sent him packing.

THE APPRENTICESHIP OF ANNIE EVA FAY
(1871)

14

Annie's infatuation with Henry outweighed any doubts she may have had about his honesty. Within months, they were married. Her new life began not with a honeymoon but with a mentorship. Henry began intensive stage-magic and spirit-conjuring training for the big stage.

Annie learned how to adapt her mediumship skills for a larger audience. Henry taught her how to perform a popular illusion known as the Spirit Cabinet. This trick had been introduced a decade earlier by the Davenport Brothers, a famed medium act from Boston. Henry changed the name of the act to the Wonder-Box. The WonderBox was a large wooden cabinet that stood seven feet high, six feet wide, and two feet deep and was balanced on sawhorses a foot above the floor. The version that Henry built most likely had a curtain in the front of the cabinet. This portion of the act was known as the **Light Séance** because it was fully lit by gaslight.

Next, Henry trained Annie for the second portion of the act. He called it the **Dark Séance** since it was performed with gaslights extinguished.

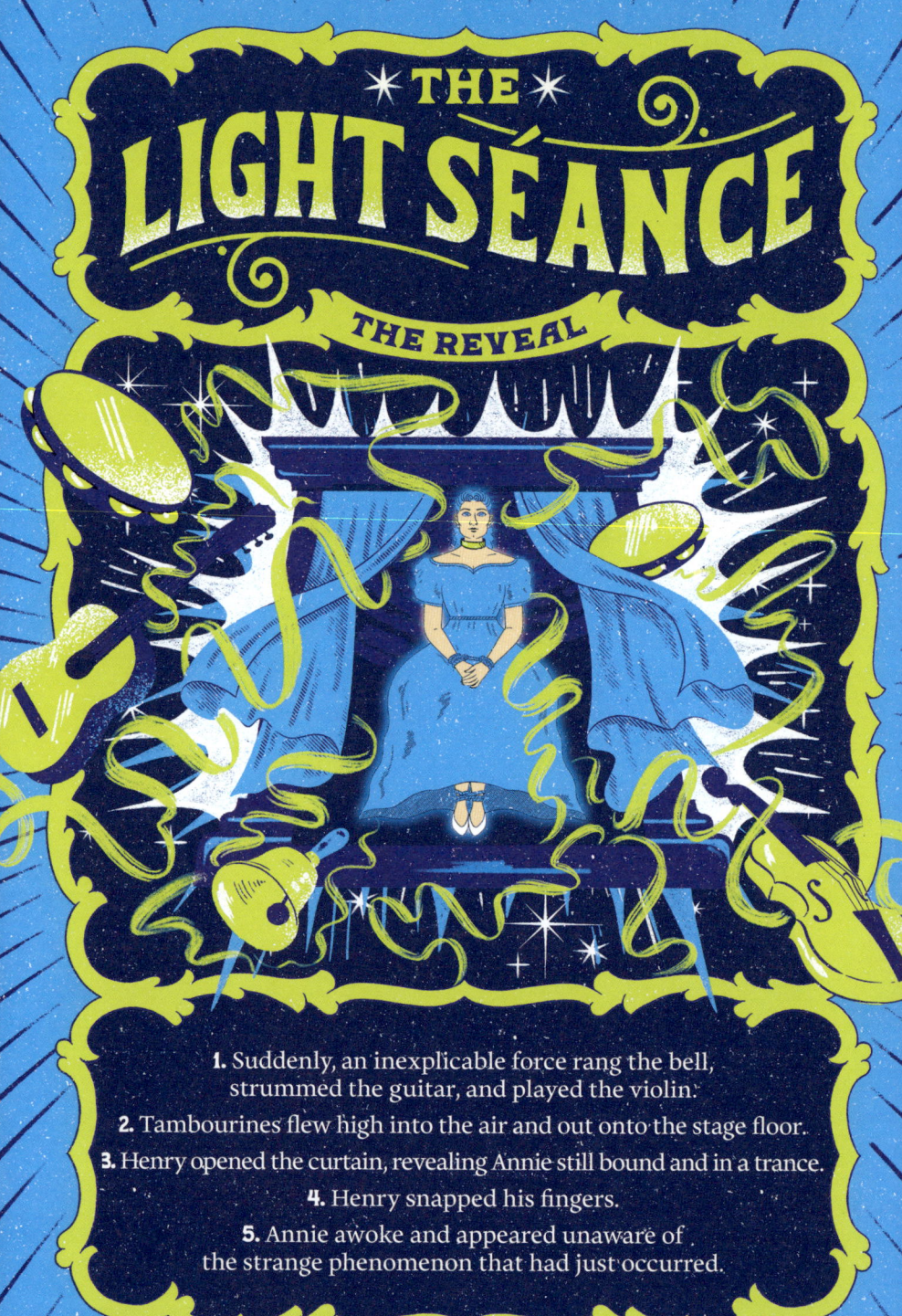

THE LIGHT SÉANCE

THE REVEAL

1. Suddenly, an inexplicable force rang the bell, strummed the guitar, and played the violin.

2. Tambourines flew high into the air and out onto the stage floor.

3. Henry opened the curtain, revealing Annie still bound and in a trance.

4. Henry snapped his fingers.

5. Annie awoke and appeared unaware of the strange phenomenon that had just occurred.

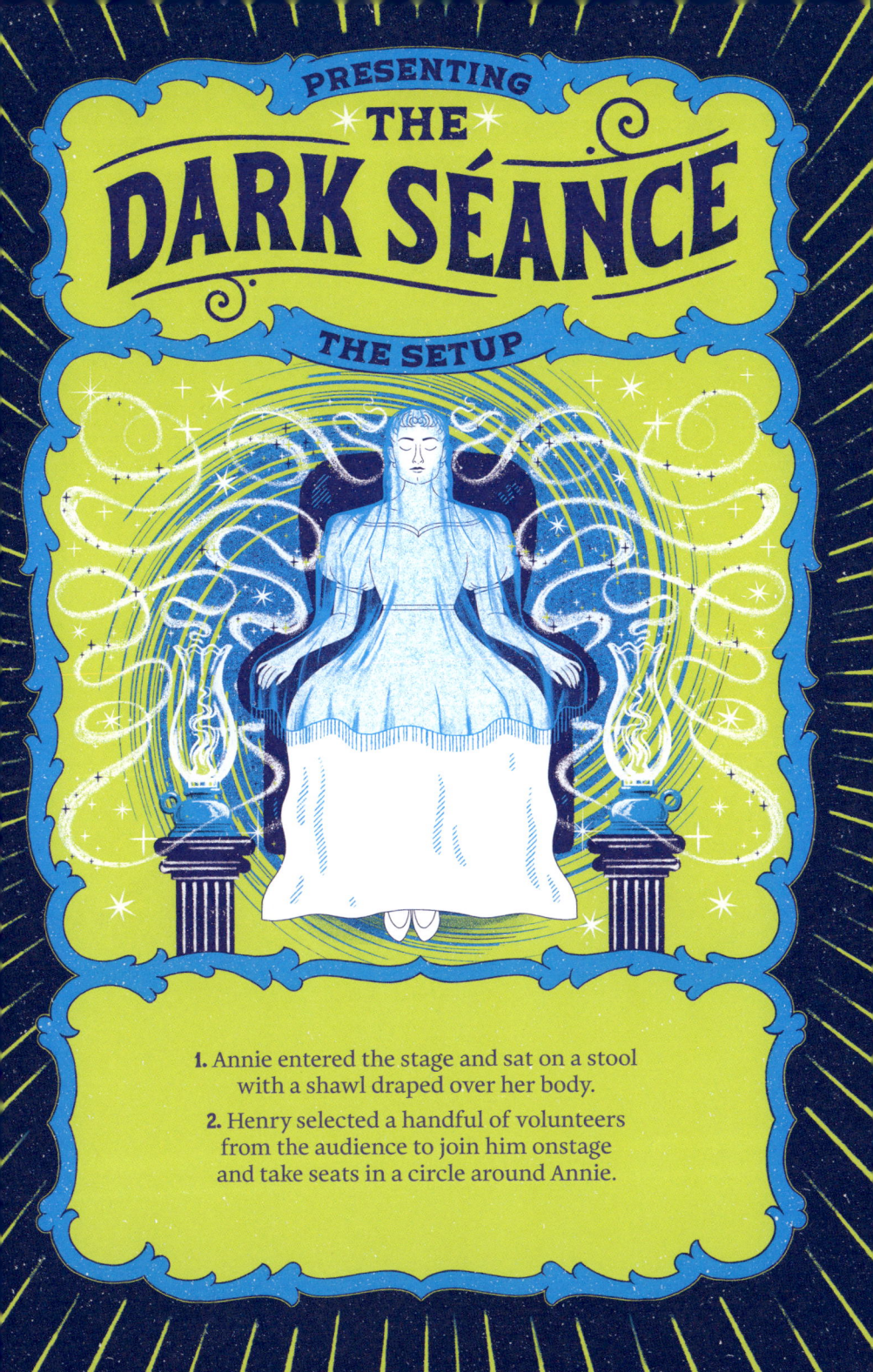

PRESENTING

THE DARK SÉANCE

THE SETUP

1. Annie entered the stage and sat on a stool with a shawl draped over her body.

2. Henry selected a handful of volunteers from the audience to join him onstage and take seats in a circle around Annie.

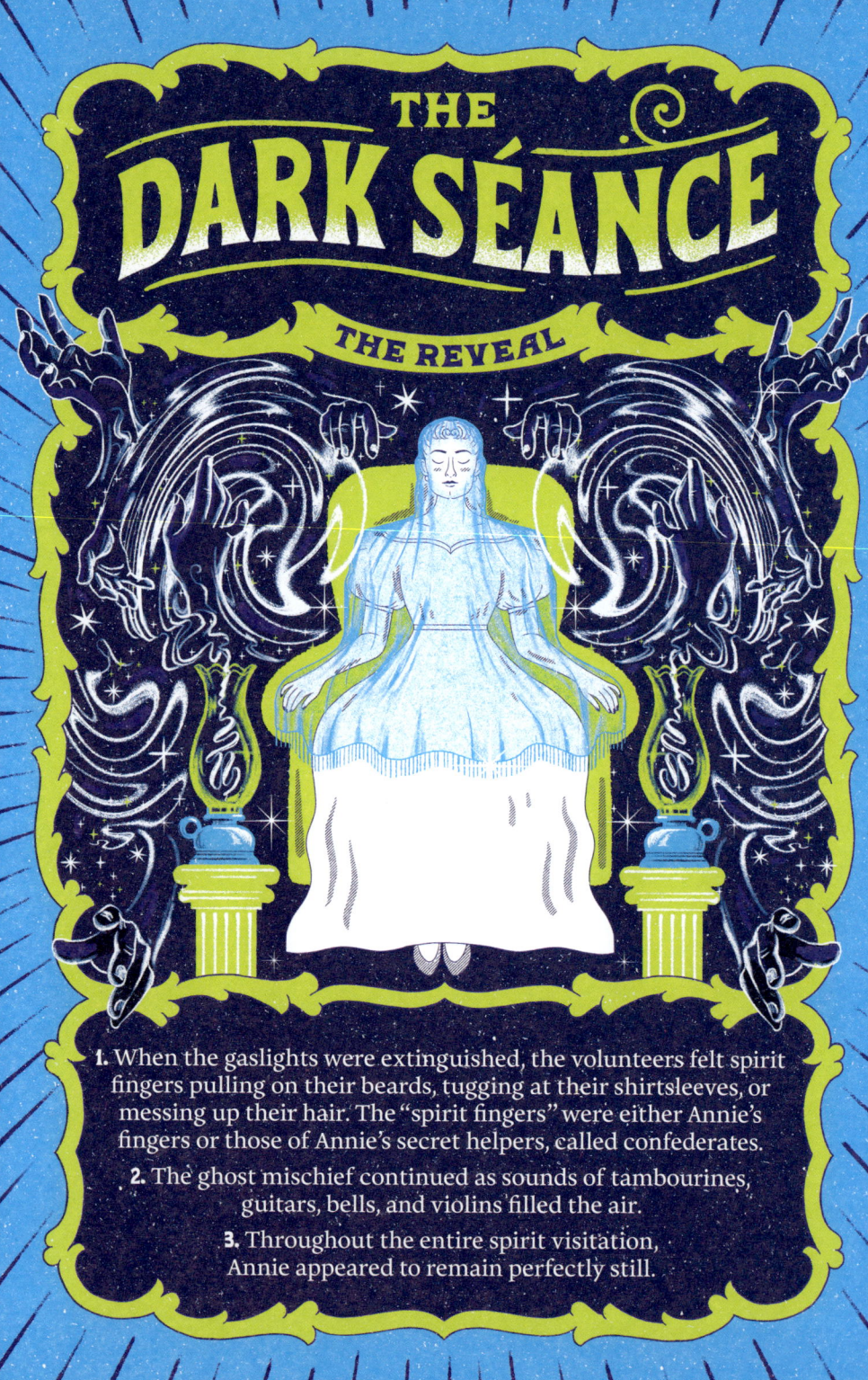

THE DARK SÉANCE

THE REVEAL

1. When the gaslights were extinguished, the volunteers felt spirit fingers pulling on their beards, tugging at their shirtsleeves, or messing up their hair. The "spirit fingers" were either Annie's fingers or those of Annie's secret helpers, called confederates.

2. The ghost mischief continued as sounds of tambourines, guitars, bells, and violins filled the air.

3. Throughout the entire spirit visitation, Annie appeared to remain perfectly still.

Henry noticed how quickly Annie adapted to the new act. She performed the visitation so convincingly that he wisely stepped aside to let his young bride shine in the spotlight, while he took on the role of master of ceremonies and manager.

THE NEW WONDER
(1874)

In 1874, Annie turned twenty-three. She had performed as a medium for more than half her life and was about to embark on her first public tour outside of the small circle of her Ohio Spiritualist supporters. "Fays' Marvelous and Sensational Manifestations" launched in Kentucky and then went to Indiana and Illinois. Glowing reviews calling the séances remarkable wonders of spirit power followed each performance. Annie's debut was well timed. She joined a new generation of female mediums who were also finding an audience. The skeptics who aimed their arrows at mediums tended to shy away from criticizing these alleged "innocents" too harshly at first. The common belief was that young women possessed an intuition that made them uniquely suited to becoming mediums.

Encouraged by the positive press, Annie and Henry

took their act to New York City and to Boston. It was in Boston that Annie's good fortune took a turn. While performing at a private séance in the upscale brownstone of a Spiritualist family, another woman medium spotted Annie creating the spirit effect. She likely had spied Annie slipping her bound hands out of the tied rope, tossing a tambourine into the air, or ringing a bell behind the curtain. The next day, the medium reported the deception to the *Boston Herald* newspaper, exposing Annie as a fraud. Annie responded by employing her charm and skill of misdirection to distract the public. She claimed that the incident was simply a matter of professional jealousy. Henry quickly booked passage to the United Kingdom, where the Fays could test their act on new audiences, far away from the controversy. This scheme of dodging skeptics also helped to keep fans guessing. Being evasive created an air of mystery. Was Annie a real medium, or was she a fake?

After a two-week steamship journey across the ocean, Annie launched her first European tour in Scotland. She performed small private séances, conjuring spirits in Spiritualist homes. Positive word of mouth led to more engagements, this time in London, England! While there, Annie performed at an exclusive press-only séance at the Crystal Palace, the same room visited by Russian emperor Alexander III just weeks before. London newspapers praised Annie. By day, she conducted private séances in a hotel room. By night, she performed on small stages around town. Her reputation as the young American wonder led to an invitation to perform at the esteemed Queen's Concert Room, better known as Queen's Hall. From her family farm in rural Ohio to the capital of the British Empire, Annie Eva Fay had arrived!

Annie's overwhelming success not only captured the attention of the British newspapers, but also the eye of English magician Nevil Maskelyne. Maskelyne and his partner, George A. Cooke, had gained attention debunking famed Spiritualist act the Davenport Brothers. Now it was Annie's turn. Maskelyne and Cooke had a significant following, so Annie needed to maintain her reputation in the eyes of her enthusiastic audiences while the magician duo publicly revealed the secrets of how her act was performed. Meanwhile, leading scientists and intellectuals took great interest in mediums. One of the most renowned scientists in London, Professor William Crookes, discoverer of the chemical element thallium and an early pioneer of atomic physics, had conducted experiments with mediums to determine if psychic phenomena truly existed. Crookes used a galvanometer to test if they in fact possessed authentic psychic power. A galvanometer was a newly invented mechanism that detected small electrical currents. Crookes invited Annie to participate in a series of these experiments. It was just the opportunity she had hoped for to distract the public from Maskelyne's exposures.

ANNIE AND THE PROFESSOR
(1875)

On the evening of February 5, 1875, Annie arrived at Crookes's residence on Mornington Road in London to conduct a private séance. First, Crookes asked Annie to hold two electrodes that were connected by wires to the galvanometer. He determined that if the electrical flow through the wires was interrupted at any point during the séance, then it would prove that she was using her body to create any spirit activity and therefore was a fraud. On the other hand, if the electrical flow was uninterrupted, then Crookes said it would prove that Annie was an authentic medium. His theory failed to take into account that Annie had a few tricks up her sleeves!

Before a small group of notable guests and with Annie's reputation on the line, the séance began. As soon as the gaslights were extinguished, a heavy musical box in the parlor opened, wound itself up, and began to play. Just as suddenly, it stopped. In another part of the room, a handbell rang on a table and dropped to the floor. In the next moment, Crookes's locked bureau opened and closed, all while Annie remained perfectly still and without any interruption to the electrical current. Using skills she had acquired as a young girl, and employing a few confederates in the room to help her with the illusion, Annie outsmarted the scientist and his intellectual colleagues, who appeared to be too enchanted by Annie's charm and beauty to notice that she had simply performed a few skillful parlor tricks.

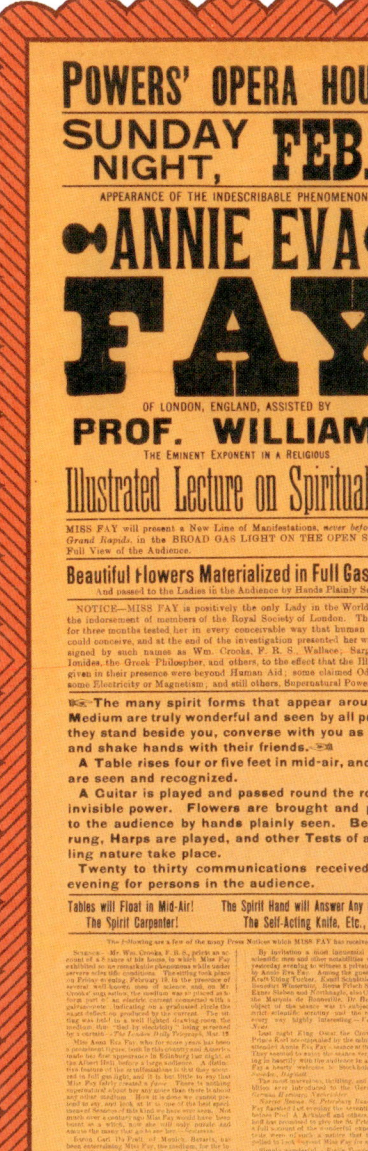

Convinced that Annie possessed the ability to contact spirits, Crookes published his findings in *The Spiritualist*, in an article entitled "A Scientific Examination of Mrs. Fay's Mediumship."

THE ENCHANTING MYSTIFIER
(1875—1889)

With the endorsement from a famed English scientist, Annie and Henry headed back to the United States. They embarked on a fresh publicity campaign. Annie renamed herself the Indescribable Phenomenon. She also changed her first name to *Anna* in an effort to sound more cosmopolitan.

In 1876, a young admirer from a Spiritualist family named Washington Irving Bishop sought out Anna while she was performing in New York City. He offered to help manage her bookings. She was flattered. In a rare instance, she let down her guard. She agreed to share her behind-the-scenes secrets with him, including how she gathered personal information about sitters and their deceased relatives and friends in each town where she performed. These trade secrets were invaluable. Both Anna and Henry trusted Bishop since he was a Spiritualist and part of the community that endorsed their act.

A few months into Bishop's employment, he demanded a share of the profits. When Anna and Henry refused, he threatened to expose them. They fired him and moved on to tour the West Coast, thinking nothing of it. Bishop made good on his threat with a series of public exposures in New York City's evening newspaper *The Daily Graphic*. The newspaper published illustrations that revealed each of Anna's tricks.

Bishop took his betrayal further by staging a live lecture at Chickering Hall, a popular venue. Before a packed house, he demonstrated, step by step, how Anna led her séances. Bishop then took Anna to court, accusing her of swindling people out of their money through trickery. Anna was forced to return to New York to face Bishop's allegations and defend herself before a judge. Her attorney enlisted a handful of influential fans of Anna's to testify on her behalf. The judge ruled that Bishop had no right to interfere with the practice of religion. That included Spiritualism. However, since Anna had profited from her particular brand of mediumship, she was required to pay a license fee. Anna never bothered to fill out the paperwork, and in the end, there appeared to be no consequences except that the ruling struck a nerve in the Spiritualist community. Each new public exposure challenged Spiritualism's core beliefs.

To get away from the gossip and controversy, Anna and Henry headed north of New York City to a sup-

portive Spiritualist community in Syracuse, New York. They hoped to put this recent round of exposures behind them, banking on distance being their friend. Life on the run was familiar to Anna and Henry. Soon they would stop running and dodging skeptics. Anna was pregnant with their first child. On May 27, 1877, she gave birth to her son, John.

But Anna couldn't afford to slow down. She needed to get back on the road. Since her absence, competition among women mediums had become fierce. She quickly landed bookings and began to tour again, with her baby in tow. For her return, she advertised herself as the Spectacular Wonder. She also added a new member to the troupe, a dashing Canadian actor named David Pingree, who posed as an English professor. David gave short lectures on Spiritualism in an attempt to bring more credibility to the act. He also brought flair, zest, and controversy. He devised outrageous publicity campaigns promising wild illusions that included thrilling levitations and flying pianos. His claims drew large crowds, but when his grand promises never materialized, outraged audiences often stormed the stage and sent the troupe packing.

The controversy didn't stop the crowds from coming to Anna's shows. The truth was that she was part performer, part magician, and part con artist. Whenever Anna was asked about her spiritual powers, she danced around the question. She may have possessed intuitive powers, although she never admitted to them. She kept journalists and audiences guessing. That was a big part of her mystique and an even bigger part of her success. To rise above the skeptics and the exposures, she coyly insisted that she was merely an entertainer and nothing more.

In 1880, while on tour, Anna discovered a dark secret. Henry was an imposter. Not only was his real name not what he said it was, but he was married to another woman! It appeared that he had "borrowed" the name Fay from a more notable magician who worked closely with the famed Davenport Brothers. He had hoped to confuse the public into thinking he was *the* Fay linked to the Davenports. Henry's last name was actually Cummings. Anna also learned that he was still married to a medium named Carrie Sawyer. Evidently, Henry had several other mistresses too. Anna wasn't about to let this betrayal steal her spotlight. Performing as a medium was all she knew. She made the shrewd business decision to keep Henry as her business partner. The tour continued, but not before Annie filed for divorce.

THE MIND READER EMERGES

(1890—1898)

By the late nineteenth century, mind reading had become all the rage. Anna quickly set to training as a mentalist to add this new bit of conjuring to her Spirit Cabinet act. She promoted herself as the Modern Oracle of Delphi and named her brand of mind reading somnolency. For this portion of her act, she sat center stage, blindfolded and wrapped in a white shawl. She answered questions from the audience with astonishing accuracy, even predicting future presidents, uncovering lost jewels, foreseeing love matches, and locating gold mines. To achieve this, she worked with troupe members who collected news and gossip from each local town. They dug into its prominent citizens' personal lives and researched select members of the audience each night. Then they delivered what they had gathered to Anna backstage before the show began. Her mind-reading skills astonished the crowds. Once again, Anna proved that she could reinvent herself as the demands and tastes of her audiences changed with the times.

While on tour in Europe, Anna received news that her father had died. She felt the pain of his loss but also the grief of their difficult relationship. His death brought back memories of her lonely childhood and her abandonment. Then Henry died from throat cancer. Even though he had betrayed Anna in marriage, she still recognized that he was the one who had taken her out of small-town Ohio and into the world. In the end, their relationship was bittersweet. If Anna had never met Henry, she might not have become a celebrated medium.

Anna chose not to attend Henry's funeral back in the States. She finished the tour with David, the handsome Canadian to whom she had grown close since Henry's betrayal. David stepped straight into Henry's role as her manager. When Anna returned to America in 1889, she bought a home outside of Boston. Using her maiden name, she called it Heathman Manor. It was a reminder of how far she had come since her childhood. After living on the road for most of her life, owning a home was a milestone for her, a symbol of security and success. Soon after she moved in, David proposed to her. They married and raised her son, John, together.

However, domestic life didn't suit Anna's restless nature. She needed the stage, to be in the spotlight, to shine. While on the road, Anna focused on her performances, which didn't provide John with a stable childhood. Yet, by bringing him with her on tour, she introduced him to the world of magic firsthand. She trained him to become her protégé and shared all her secrets with him. John mastered the rapping spirit hand trick that Anna had added to her repertoire, in which a wooden hand on a pedestal mysteriously rapped out answers to questions from the audience. He also played the role of a uniformed attendant who gathered information about the audience for Anna's mind-reading act. By the time he turned sixteen, he knew his mother's act inside and out.

FAMILY DRAMA
(1898—1908)

In 1898, while on tour in St. Louis, twenty-one-year-old John met a performer named Eva Jean Norman. She was a towering beauty who was twelve years older than him. They fell in love and ran off to get married. Within weeks, the newlyweds resurfaced onstage with an act called the Marvelous Fays. While the duo was new to the public, their act was anything but—Anna discovered that John and Eva had stolen her entire act! John behaved as though he had resented living in his mother's shadow all these years. He believed that it was his turn to take the spotlight. The couple further betrayed Anna by copying her mind-reading performance, naming their version Thaumaturgy. Anna had sold copper collectible mascots with her initials embossed on them at her shows, while John and Eva sold similar copper mascots with only the slightest design variation. The relentless imitation and betrayal continued. When Anna wrote a book about her interpretations of dream symbolism, Eva Fay wrote her own dream book, calling it *The Fay Thaumaturgy Dream Book*. Anna claimed in her advertisements that she was 80 percent accurate with her mind reading. Eva Fay claimed to be 85 percent accurate. This family drama reached fever pitch when Anna and Eva and John performed the same week in New York City at competing nearby venues. The headline in *Vanity Fair*'s gossip column read "Furious Fay Fight, Farcically Frenzied, Furnishes Fun Freely." John fueled the fire by sending a public message to his mother: "It is time for you to retire, O Mother! Make way for the young and wise!"

Despite John's rebellion and deceit, Anna still loved her son. Distraught over their growing conflict, Anna tried to make peace. She purchased a small house for him on the property next to Heathman Manor. She furnished it and even deposited a large sum of money into a bank account in his name. It's unclear why the rift had developed, but it can be surmised that Anna had spent more time pursuing fame and fortune than nurturing her only son. Eva Norman also appeared to have a bewitching influence over John. She publicly exploited the mother-son relationship and created a painful feud between them for her own personal gain.

Anna kept performing despite her grief. She was now part of a larger vaudeville tour circuit with a variety of stage performers. By the late 1890s, vaudeville had evolved into the most popular form of entertainment in America. It reflected a cross-section of the culture and the tastes of the time. The bill usually included lighthearted comedy, dancing, singing, cowboy stunts, and circus acts. Anna adapted quickly to this new theatrical format and thrived. By the early 1900s, she had become the highest paid entertainer in vaudeville!

Then tragedy struck. John died by suicide. He didn't leave a note, and it was never explained. Although Anna found it difficult to recover from the loss, she carried on performing. In 1913, London's preeminent magic society, The Magic Circle, invited her to join its ranks. She was the first woman to become an honorary lady associate. Celebrated magician Harry Houdini knew of her achievements and called her the greatest mystifier of her day. Around this time, Harry and Anna began a cordial letter correspondence. Anna had reached the peak of her career. In 1920, she was approaching seventy years old. Her act had become even more spectacular, with bizarre antics, sensational advertising, and off-the-wall publicity stunts; she even claimed that she believed there was life on Mars. She also theorized that humans were reincarnated onto other planets and insisted that she could astral-project across countries. She now promoted herself as the Psychic Marvel of the Twentieth Century, with the slogan "Ask Anna Eva Fay. She knows everything." Her new title came with a disclaimer: "Note, Mrs. Fay gives no private audiences. She is not a fortune teller, palmist, or pretender. She is purely an entertainer." To stay competitive, Anna switched roles from medium to magician and from entertainer to mystic.

Meanwhile, popular entertainment in the country was turning its attention west, away from the vaudeville stage toward Hollywood and silent movies. The golden age of magic was fading away, making room for the rise of a new attraction: the movie star. Anna had survived skeptics and critics throughout her career. In the end, her biggest competition seemed to have been a world moving faster than she could keep up with. In 1918, Anna Eva Fay announced she would embark on her farewell tour. The tour lasted

almost six years. In 1924, after a performance in Milwaukee, Anna fell and badly injured her leg. Days later, she announced her retirement and retreated to Heathman Manor.

AN UNEXPECTED VISITOR
(1924)

While recovering at home, Anna received a letter. It was from Harry Houdini, requesting a personal visit. Harry and Anna had maintained their casual letter exchange for over a decade, but they had never met. Over this time,

Harry had developed a special interest in mediums after losing his mother. Since her passing in 1913, he visited more than one hundred mediums in hopes of receiving a message from her spirit. None of the séances yielded a sign. His grief turned to anger. He staged an all-out attack on mediums, accusing them of taking advantage of those who were in pain and in mourning. He even targeted Anna in his book *A Magician Among the Spirits*, in which he exposed her tricks. The book was published just weeks before his letter arrived at Anna's door.

Anna agreed to Harry's visit, graciously forgiving him for his public attacks. She defended him to other mediums and professional magician friends. Even in retirement, Anna didn't truly stop working, and here, she saw an opportunity. Always savvy when it came to publicity, she knew that a visit from the world's most famous magician would bring intrigue and maybe even a headline. Harry was in Boston preparing to expose another charismatic female medium, a young socialite named Mina Crandon who called herself Margery the Medium. Perhaps that was his motivation. Maybe Harry thought that since Anna had retired, she would reveal her secrets to him and coach him for his latest exposure of a medium. Maybe Anna would finally admit that her act was nothing more than a series of well-orchestrated magic tricks.

On a hot, muggy New England summer day in July 1924, Anna and Harry shared six hours of conversation at Heathman Manor. Houdini claimed that Anna revealed all her secrets to him that day, including how she fooled Professor Crookes during the galvanometer experiments. Anna coyly denied revealing anything. After the visit, when asked if she had confessed to her deceptions, she answered the question with another question, "How can I admit to something that never happened?"

During the visit, Anna and Harry discovered a connection they shared besides a life of magic: grief over a loved one. Anna, for her son, John. And Harry, for his mother, Cecilia. After the visit, their letters took on a more personal tone. Harry died less than two years later

at the age of fifty-two. For Anna, his untimely death meant the loss of a crucial link to the magic world and her illustrious past.

THE FAREWELL

(1924—1927)

Anna died seven months after Houdini, on May 12, 1927. David inherited the estate, along with Anna's large unpaid debts. Toward the end of her life, Anna's wealth had diminished, but her spending had not. She was buried next to her son, John, in the family mausoleum near Heathman Manor. The press reported on her passing, but there was no record of a funeral. This notorious, one-of-a-kind, risk-taking, rule-breaking, groundbreaking woman magician . . . *vanished.*

zet you...
hoping you are well
and all is well you...
... Fay

ADELAIDE HERRMANN

QUEEN of MAGIC

THE PERFORMER

AUGUST 11, 1853 – FEBRUARY 19, 1932

YOUNG ADDIE STEPS INTO THE WORLD

1853–1870

As a girl, Adelaide Herrmann dreamed she could fly. She wondered how it would feel to lift into the air and watch the world from above. *How magical it would be,* she thought, *to soar through the sky like a bird!* Adelaide was born two years after Anna Eva Fay, on August 11, 1853. Her birth name was Adele Scarsez. Unlike Anna, who was born into poverty, Adelaide's parents were Belgian immigrants who built a comfortable life for their family in London, England. In the 1850s, Queen Victoria ruled over Britain's vast empire. London was a city of contradictions, of great wealth and extreme poverty. Adelaide's father thrived and had many business investments. One of them, the Egyptian Hall, was a lively entertainment stage for popular magicians and other cultural institutions. It would play a key role in Adelaide's incredible life as a woman magician.

Each theater season, Addie waited impatiently for the pantomime shows to arrive in town. Pantomime was an extremely popular form of theater in Victorian England, performed mostly without speaking. Instead, the shows featured well-known fairy tales, nursery rhymes, and myths told through lively music, exaggerated humor, and colorful costumes. The shows were performed in front of dazzling sets. Stock characters poked fun at the ruling class and the high-society lifestyle that eluded most Londoners. These over-the-top characters contrasted with the quiet and polite behavior expected of proper young girls growing up in cosmopolitan London. Adelaide loved it! When she wasn't dreaming about the theatrics of pantomime, she insisted that her parents take her to the traveling circus. The spectacle, the colors, and the magic of the big top performances inspired her. She especially enjoyed the trapeze artists, who flew through the air effortlessly and joyously. She could hardly contain her secret wish to become a part of this extraordinary world. One morning, she spotted an advertisement in a London newspaper, seeking young girls to apply for a dance school led by a notable Hungarian performance troupe, the Kiralfy Brothers. This was Addie's chance to step into a world that she had only dreamed of.

The next day, young Addie snuck out of her house. She auditioned and landed a coveted spot in the troupe! From the start, Madame Kiralfy, one of the sisters in the family-run company, saw great promise in Addie. As for Addie, she immediately fell in love with dance. In those moments when she leaped across the floor, she felt closer to her dream of flight. At night, her body ached from the long hours of practice, but she kept her secret to herself. Life onstage was not what Addie's parents envisioned for their beautiful and spirited daughter. They had other plans for her: to find a husband, create a family, run a household. Addie had a different idea. As the weeks passed, it became harder for her to continue the deception. When she finally shared it with her sister and her best friend, they were thrilled. They made a pact to not only help hide Addie's secret, but insisted they join the class too!

A few months later, Madame Kiralfy selected Addie to join the traveling professional dance company. The Kiralfy Brothers had just booked a tour in the United States, and there was a spot in the show for an extra dancer. It was 1868. Addie was about to turn sixteen. She needed her parents' approval to travel across the Atlantic to perform in America. She gathered her courage and confessed to them. Before her parents would agree, they demanded to see her perform. After seeing Addie featured in the ballet *The Fairy Roses* the following week, they couldn't deny her talent or her ambition. They allowed her to travel with the troupe under Madame Kiralfy's supervision. Addie's dream was coming true.

In America, Addie performed a variety of dance numbers, including a high-kick version of the famed cancan, in which dancers raised their skirts to show their legs and kicked high into the sky. It was a scandalous dance brought to America from Europe. The New York audience loved it! Addie was in her element, frolicking around New York City and dancing in front of a live audience. She continued to Boston with a small group of dancers who called themselves the Deardon Sisters. While high-kicking and ballet dancing in Boston, Adelaide attracted the attention of popular vaudeville comedian Gus Williams, the American Star Comique. They struck up a romance. After only a few weeks of courtship, Gus proposed. Addie needed her parents' permission before going forward with the marriage. Madly in love, she boarded the next cross-Atlantic steamer back to London.

While at home, the letters from Gus became fewer and fewer, until Adelaide finally called off the engagement. To cheer her up, a friend invited her to the matinee of a magic show at the Egyptian Hall. It was the perfect distraction for Addie, who was nursing a broken heart. The show featured an exciting new French magician named Alexander Herrmann. For one shilling, you could see Alexander perform a series of spectacular sleight of hand tricks, the type of magic trick where the visual deceptions are created using only a magicians' hands. Alexander might have produced an endless stream of cards that emerged from a bouquet of flowers, or revealed a bowl of live goldfish out of thin air, or even pulled a rabbit out of his top hat. He would have strolled through the audience performing these close-up tricks while telling entertaining stories with his spontaneous sharp tongue and clever wit. His piercing eyes and formal dress—black suit and tails, waxed mustache curled at the sides, and a pointy goatee—created an iconic look that would define his illustrious career.

Addie had never seen anyone like Alexander. Who was this gifted and handsome magician? At one point during the performance, Alexander looked out into the crowd and asked, "Are there any ladies in the audience who would lend me her ring?" Addie looked down at the engagement ring she still wore. Without thinking, she raised her hand. One of Alexander's attendants scooped up the ring and brought it onstage, where Alexander promptly set it on fire! Or did he? Within a few minutes,

a lily-white dove flew down into the audience, heading straight toward Addie's seat. There was the ring hanging on a ribbon around its neck. Addie quickly untied the ribbon and placed the ring back on her finger. After the show, Addie's friend brought her backstage to meet the mysterious conjurer. The two were cordial to each other, and the meeting appeared to be of no real significance. Or so Addie thought.

THE PERFORMER ARRIVES
(1870–1875)

Adelaide put her romantic troubles behind her and returned to performing. She decided to teach herself to ride the velocipede, a trendy high-wheeled bicycle that had become hugely popular in Victorian England in the 1870s. After mastering the skill, she joined a group of all-women trick riders called Professor Brown's Lady Velocipede Troupe. They launched their act in Paris at the famed Folies Bergère. The performance was the first of its kind and an instant hit. Soon Addie was performing bike tricks on stages throughout Europe. Her love and talent for dance transformed once again, this time on a bicycle six feet in the air! She performed acrobatics and ballet moves on a bicycle seat. As the finale, the troupe linked arms while riding in unison around the stage to music from a small orchestra.

During one performance, Adelaide lost her balance and fell into the orchestra pit below the stage. She claimed the mishap only added more comedy to the show! She got right back on the bike and finished the act to a standing ovation. An American booking agent seeking new novelty acts hired the all-women velocipede troupe to perform for his vaudeville stage shows in New York and Boston. At twenty-one, when most young women were marrying and keeping house, Adelaide was packing her costume trunk to board a steamship for her second trip to America. Her dream of dancing had not only developed into a passion but had blossomed into a promising career in vaudeville.

On the morning of departure, Adelaide watched excitedly from the steamer's railing as the final passengers boarded the ship. Suddenly a commotion erupted. A path cleared for a man wearing a fashionable fur coat and sporting a top hat. *He must be a prince!* thought Adelaide. When she spied the waxed mustache that curled at the sides and the pointy goatee, she knew who it was—the charming magician with the piercing eyes and the larger-than-life presence—Monsieur Alexander Herrmann. Since Adelaide had attended his magic show at the Egyptian Hall almost six years earlier, Alexander had set a record by performing there for 1,000 nights. In that time, he had emerged as one of the most famous and respected magicians in the world. He now called himself Herrmann the Great.

The two-week voyage led to a maritime flirtation between Adelaide and Alexander. It began when Adelaide first reintroduced herself to him. He insisted that he remembered their backstage encounter. From that moment on, he couldn't keep his eyes off her. He invited her to dine with him at the captain's table. He sent her gifts—champagne and delicacies from the ship's kitchen. They spent evenings strolling on the deck, enjoying the sea air, lounging on the deck chairs, and engaging in conversation in French. Alexander even played an April Fool's joke by sending out a steward to announce that he had slipped and broken his leg. It was Adelaide who was first to come to his rescue. By the end of the journey, the two had fallen in love.

Once on America's shores, they divided their time between New York City and Boston. After almost a year of courtship, Alexander proposed. They were married in a civil ceremony in New York City, but not before Alexander announced to the mayor that he had no money to pay for it. After a few awkward moments, Alexander deftly pulled a roll of dollar bills out from the mayor's long beard to pay for the license. This was just one example of the fun that Herrmann the Great would bring to a shared life of magic with Adelaide.

ADELAIDE AND ALEXANDER
(1875—1896)

Adelaide embarked on her new life as a young bride with her celebrated magician husband. She took on the role with the same grace and poise she had displayed onstage as a dancer. She and Alexander began their marriage as equal partners and both had a voice in the direction of their shows. The new act blended

their talents. Alexander expanded his sleight of hand magic into larger-scale illusions. Inspired by her childhood passion for pantomime and the circus, Adelaide added theatrics and spectacle to their performances. She also brought a grand vision to the show by commissioning original music, employing a small orchestra, designing lighting effects, choreographing dances, and creating eye-catching, sparkly, talked-about costumes every season.

Most of this was behind the curtain, though. Onstage, Adelaide was Alexander's chief assistant—but she was dressed as a man! She was his body double, cutting her hair short and wearing a long-tailed black jacket and a high-collared white shirt. At the time, women assistants didn't walk through the audience collecting handkerchiefs, jewelry, and watches to use as props in their now-you-see-it-now-you-don't sleight of hand tricks. It was more customary for female assistants to remain onstage as mysterious beauties to admire, not to dress as men and swipe valuables from audience members to make them disappear!

Adelaide couldn't contain her ambition or her talent for very long. She quickly evolved from assistant to performer. One of the first acts that featured her as the star attraction poked fun at mediums, who Adelaide believed faked spirit visitations and fooled their audiences for a profit. She performed magic to entertain, not to deceive. She and Alexander developed an act mocking popular Spiritualist mediums, calling it "Ten Minutes with Modern Spirits." The act re-created a spirit cabinet, similar to the one Anna Eva Fay featured in her act. The spirits appeared as skeletons dancing onstage. When the lights were turned up, it was revealed that they were actually dancers performing a lighthearted show. The message to the audience was that spirit visitation was just entertainment, not the mysterious phenomenon that mediums wanted them to believe.

As bookings started rolling in, Adelaide and Alexander felt the pressure to outdo themselves. Vaudeville had gained popularity. Cities grew, and variety shows spread to smaller towns across the country. The demand for acts was greater, but so was the competition. While Alexander still performed sleight of hand tricks, pulling rabbits out of hats and making gentlemen's watches disappear, the Herrmanns continually transformed their act. They needed to keep up with the times. Adelaide added unique touches too, taking her dances to new heights.

The trick that defined them during this period was a groundbreaking levitation illusion called the **Aerial Suspension**.

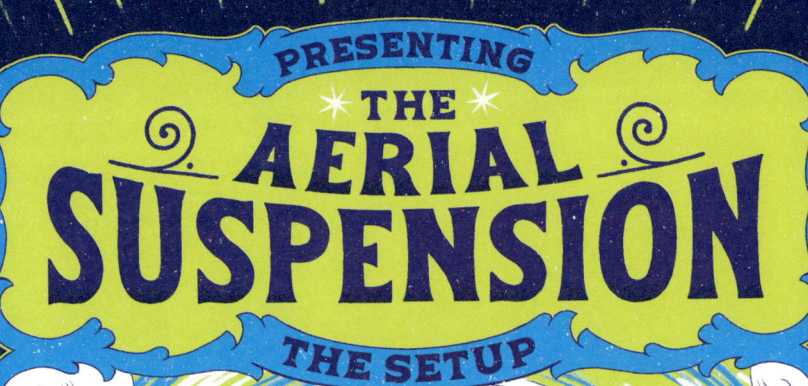

PRESENTING
THE
AERIAL
SUSPENSION
THE SETUP

1. A small stool was placed on a platform.

2. Adelaide entered the stage in a flowing white robe.

3. Alexander guided her onto the platform and then the stool.

4. He took two long metal poles and placed them under her arms.

5. He held an ether-soaked handkerchief under Adelaide's nose.

6. Adelaide quickly fell into a deep sleep.

THE AERIAL SUSPENSION

THE REVEAL

1. Music began as Adelaide slept. Alexander took away one of the poles and fanned a palm leaf that lifted Adelaide into the air.

2. As she floated, he placed her in picturesque poses.

3. He then positioned the pole back under Adelaide's arm and fanned her back down onto the stool.

4. Alexander waved his hands around her until she awoke, appearing unaware of what had just happened.

Alexander taught Adelaide more than how to fly. He mentored her in illusions where she blossomed into a star. She learned how to disappear, reappear, and catch fire in her bare hands. In one popular illusion, the Artist's Dream, a young painter falls in love with the woman in his painting. Suddenly Alexander, dressed as the devil, appears and brings the painted woman, played by Adelaide, to life. Then Alexander's devil character makes her disappear back into the painting to the heartbreak of the young love-stricken artist. The illusion created a sensation!

Adelaide never stopped developing the act and her role in it. As gas-powered lighting became commonplace in theaters, she took full advantage of the development by choreographing dances utilizing lighting effects. She fashioned extreme costumes, occasionally using more than thirty feet of fabric in a single dress to simulate butterflies in flight, dancing fire, and flowers that bloomed before the audience's eyes. She performed against a black velvet curtain for dramatic effect. Adelaide began a typical show by performing a series of tricks and illusions with Alexander. Then she would take the stage solo, as a dancer, where her passion for movement and fanciful costumes were on full display. Her serpentine dances generated great excitement. For these dances, Adelaide wore a dress made of black chiffon

with flashing steel spangles. She would glide and slither around the stage, creating the effect of a giant serpent.

The overwhelming demand for Alexander and Adelaide's performances led them around the world. Life on the road in the late 1880s and 1890s was not easy, even for notable magicians. Adelaide and Alexander, along with their troupe and trained animals, took long train rides throughout America and weeks-long steamship voyages to Europe. In South America, Mexico, and Cuba, where there were no trains for them to board, they traveled by carriage or horseback. Sometimes they even rode on stagecoaches along winding dirt roads, through narrow streams, and over treacherous mountains! Throughout it all, the couple relished the beauty of the different cultures and embraced the customs of the places they visited. Wherever they performed, they collected gifts of silver and gold, pottery, silks, and clothing. While in Mexico and South America, they often performed under starry skies to spirited and appreciative audiences. Invariably, following each show, they shared late-night dinners highlighted by table magic, local food, and lively conversation with the most famous personalities of the time, including presidents, kings, and queens. Adelaide collected animals along the way too, including a menagerie of ostriches, horses, birds, and dogs. She not only cast them in the act, but some became her personal pets. Adelaide once adopted a ring-tailed monkey she named Jimmie that she brought on tour as her traveling companion.

While touring Venezuela, a trapeze artist who performed a new attraction called the Cannon Ball Trick suddenly quit the show. Adelaide volunteered to perform the trick herself. Alexander hesitated at first, fearing the potential danger. After Adelaide's persuasion, he finally agreed. She got to work training for the trick. Her childhood dream of flight was further realized when she was shot fifty feet out of a cannon that evening. Her only complaints after performing the trick were the loud sounds of the cannon, the smell of gunpowder, and the burns on the bottom of her feet!

Of all the roles that Adelaide played in her partnership with Alexander, the most challenging was trying to keep up with his extravagant tastes and excessive spending. Even with their overwhelming success and fame, they

still lived performance to performance, relying on the paycheck from their next booking to keep them afloat. Amid the rising costs of the productions, they threw caution to the wind and decided to buy their first home. They called it Whitestone Manor. It sat on eighteen acres on the picturesque Long Island Sound in New York. Whitestone Manor served as their retreat from the hustle and bustle, a destination for socializing and mixing with other magicians and friends. It boasted nineteen rooms, including nine bedrooms.

On the grounds, there was a large vegetable garden that Adelaide tended to, a variety of carriages for Alexander's six horses that were boarded in the manor's stable, and a set of rowboats docked by the shore. Alexander added to his spending spree by purchasing a 107-foot yacht he called *Fra Diavolo* ("among the devil" in Italian). It was a clever nod to his onstage persona. Peacocks, geese, goats, a pair of Chihuahuas, a pointer, and a Great Dane freely roamed the property. To add to the eccentricities, Alexander planted all varieties of tricks inside and outside the house. When guests arrived, the front gate inexplicably opened and closed unattended. While dining, silverware miraculously appeared on the dining table in front of guests just before dinner was served. If a guest requested a cigar, a drawer opened on command, displaying Cuba's finest. Bells rang and music played from invisible sources throughout the house.

Alexander expanded his investments at this time, placing his earnings into theaters in Philadelphia and New York. His most prized possession was the private train car that he named Herrmann's Railcar. For performances in the United States, Adelaide and Alexander hitched their private train car to commercial trains, and off they traveled to their next engagement. They customized the railcar to fit their lifestyle and to suit Alexander's vision of luxury travel. The walls were built from oak panels, the seats were covered with fine leather, and silk curtains hung in each of the cabins. In the bathroom, Alexander even installed a silverplated bathtub!

Adelaide lived a charmed and unconventional life with Alexander. As a young Londoner who dreamed of dance and flight, she could not have imagined the adventures that would unfold with Herrmann the Great by her side. Even though she enjoyed her nieces and nephews who frequently visited the Manor, she never had children. Adelaide lived her life as an independent and fearless woman of magic.

THE LAST TRAIN RIDE

(1896)

After a benefit performance in Rochester, New York, and a night out with friends, Alexander retreated to his bedroom cabin for a night's rest. That following morning on December 17, 1896, while heading to the next booking in Bradford, Pennsylvania, Alexander succumbed to a sudden heart attack at the age of fifty-two. He died in Adelaide's arms. Devastated, Adelaide didn't know where to turn. She tried to imagine a life without Alexander but couldn't. Still on the train, she transported Alexander's body to New York City. On the way, she noticed that the birds whose cages hung around Alexander's bedroom were unusually quiet. She discovered that an assistant had covered them out of respect for Alexander's passing. Adelaide knew that Alexander would have loved to hear the sounds of their singing, so asked that the birdcages be un-covered so the birds could serenade him on his last train ride.

At forty-three years old, Adelaide had lost her one true love. But as a performer, she had no time to mourn. After Alexander was laid to rest in Woodlawn Cemetery in the Bronx, New York, she faced piling debts and had both troupe members and dozens of stage animals to support. She needed to fulfill her contract and finish the tour. She telegrammed Alexander's look-a-like nephew, Leon Herrmann, who was also a magician, and asked if he would take on Alexander's role. He boarded the next ocean steamer to New York. Adelaide began training him as soon as he arrived. Although a talented magician, Leon didn't possess the genius and wit of Alexander. Addie gave him top billing since the tour had been booked with the expectation that Alexander would be headlining. Leon not only looked like Alexander, but he shared the same name. Adelaide drew the line at allowing Leon to call himself Herrmann the Great. Instead, she renamed the act Herrmann the Great Co. and declared her role as prestidigitrice. Prestidigitator is another word for a magician. Its origins come from the Latin word *praestigiae*, which means magic performance and illusion. Adelaide decided to tweak the word and give it a feminine twist.

The new show was based on Alexander and Adelaide's former act and divided into two parts. Leon performed sleight of hand magic in the first section, while part two featured Adelaide's beautifully choreographed dances. Adelaide also added a new routine for her return to the stage: A Night in Japan. The tricks included conjuring roses from thin air and making billiard balls magically appear and disappear before the audience's eyes. All this was performed in pantomime with only

musical accompaniment. Adelaide was ready to perform again just three weeks after the tragic morning on Herrmann's Railcar.

Adelaide carefully staged her debut by renting the prestigious Metropolitan Opera House for $1,800, a large sum for the time. To add to the spectacle, she planned to perform a trick no other woman had ever performed onstage. Even most male magicians wouldn't dare. It was called the **Bullet Catch**. A trick Alexander promised Adelaide he'd only perform for charity. And when he did, Adelaide hid in her dressing room until it was over. Performing one of the most dangerous tricks in magic sent a message that Madame Adelaide Herrmann was back, stronger than ever, and ready to take on the world of magic on her own terms.

As the curtain rose and the orchestra played the same Strauss waltz that Alexander used for his opening trick, Adelaide became overcome by emotion. She gathered herself and, with Leon, made her entrance to a packed house.

PRESENTING

THE
BULLET CATCH

THE SETUP

1. Six uniformed veterans marched onstage with rifles.

2. Adelaide followed.

3. The veterans laid the cartridges from their ammunition belts onto a metal plate.

4. The bullets were passed to the audience for inspection, then carried back onstage.

5. The marksmen loaded their rifles, formed two lines, and knelt down, each on one knee.

THE
BULLET CATCH

THE REVEAL

1. The sergeant shouted for all to hear, "Are you ready?"

2. Adelaide nodded, then lifted a small metal plate in front of her face.

3. The militiamen raised their rifles and aimed at Adelaide.

4. The sergeant yelled, "Fire!" The rifles went off with a loud bang, followed by the smell of gunpowder.

5. Adelaide showed the audience six bullets on the metal plate, creating the illusion that she had caught them all!

But after only three seasons together, Adelaide and Leon parted ways. There was no love lost between them, especially when Leon went against Adelaide's wishes and publicized himself as Herrmann the Great for his solo performances. Adelaide made other changes in her life too. She sold Whitestone Manor, along with Alexander's yacht and a number of their prized possessions. As much as it pained her, she also gave up Herrmann's Railcar. Then she gathered the belongings that she hadn't auctioned off and stored them a warehouse in downtown New York City.

It was the late 1890s and a turning point for Adelaide. She needed to reinvent herself with a newly imagined solo show. A woman headlining a large-scale magic show had no precedent. That didn't stop Addie. She refused to let the grief and heartbreak of losing her beloved Alexander slow her down. She soon discovered that performing magic was healing for her. The awe and wonder she created for her audiences lifted her spirits. Adelaide needed the stage to survive. Performing magic helped her carry on.

Her first official solo booking was in Chicago, where she performed in pantomime inspired by the shows she had seen in London as a young girl. Performing to music without words was also a clever business strategy when touring internationally. No need for translation for a show that relied solely on visual illusions and dramatic dances. Adelaide combined parts of the act that she and Alexander had performed together with new illusions that were distinctly her own. The show was a success. She emerged once again as a star, crowned by the press as the Queen of Magic. After receiving rave reviews in Chicago, she took her show to New York, then on to Europe. While in England, in honor of King Edward VII's upcoming coronation in 1902, she resurrected an act that Alexander had performed called Flags of All Nations. The act began by lighting a piece of paper and throwing it into the air. From the flames, hundreds of international flags appeared, each increasing in size until only two large flags remained. The American and British ones. The illusion was performed to one of Britain's most patriotic songs, "Rule, Britannia!" The English public loved it.

During the offseason, while rummaging through old props and set pieces wondering which act she would revive next, Adelaide stumbled upon an illusion that had been packed away long ago. It struck her that she could perform it in a new way. It became one of Adelaide's most popular illusions as a solo artist.

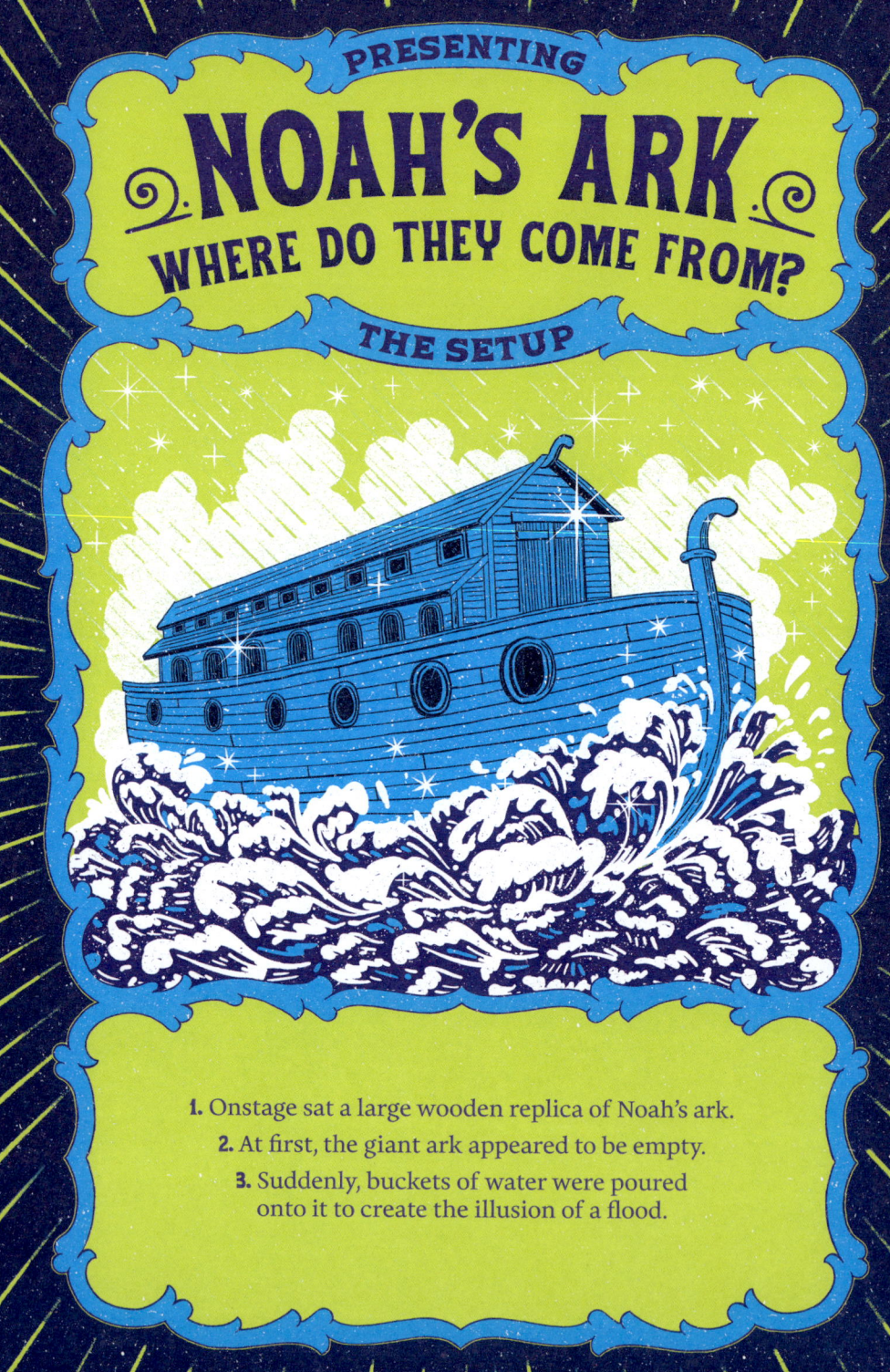

PRESENTING
NOAH'S ARK
WHERE DO THEY COME FROM?
THE SETUP

1. Onstage sat a large wooden replica of Noah's ark.
2. At first, the giant ark appeared to be empty.
3. Suddenly, buckets of water were poured onto it to create the illusion of a flood.

NOAH'S ARK
WHERE DO THEY COME FROM?

THE REVEAL

1. Two cats, one black and one white, climbed out from the ark and sauntered down the opened plank.

2. Next, a parade of birds appeared, waddling side by side.

3. Pairs of leopards, lions, tigers, zebras, and elephants then emerged. The wild animals were actually trained dogs in costume!

4. A flock of white doves suddenly flew out of the ark's windows.

5. Finally, the ark opened to reveal a beautiful woman casually lounging inside, dressed in an ethereal white dress.

Could it be that Adelaide chose this act since it resonated with her own miraculous journey of navigating and surviving rough waters and emerging to tell her story?

Adelaide was a survivor. Male magicians at the time, such as Harry Houdini, Harry Kellar, and Howard Thurston, all praised her contribution to the magic community. She had no equal at the time. In 1904, The Society of American Magicians inducted her into their esteemed organization.

Adelaide never stopped inventing and performing. She continued to tour America, arranging her own travel and organizing the transport of her show's sets, props, and costumes. At times, she performed sixty weeks in a row, adding to and refining the illusions and dances, always creating, never satisfied. As she grew older, she took on more classic women's roles, such as those of Joan of Arc and Cleopatra. One of her favorites was the levitation illusion where she made a young bride vanish. She called it the Phantom Bride. She also performed an illusion in which she dressed as an old woman who is reborn as a young dancer. The act reflected Adelaide's own reality of facing middle age and yearning for her lost carefree youth.

THE FIRE

(1926)

On the morning September 7, 1926, Adelaide was awakened by a phone call. The warehouse where she stored all her sets, props, animals, and most valuable possessions, including her wedding silver and mementos collected over the years with Alexander, had caught fire. A suspected illegal alcohol distillery was to blame. By the time Adelaide arrived, the building was consumed by flames. The firefighters delivered the news that all Adelaide's animals had perished. Then she looked up to discover her cat, Magic, teetering on a ledge. She called out to her. The cat leaped down on command. Adelaide later found her white poodle, Mamie, and her terrier, Nellie, alive too. But those were the only survivors among the over sixty trained animals she traveled with for her stage show. Gone too were her illusions, including the famed Noah's ark set pieces. The only set that had been salvaged was for an act called Sleeping Beauty. A few weeks later, when it was safe to enter the warehouse to review the damage, Adelaide discovered that the illusion had been stolen by scavengers. She was devastated. She wondered what Alexander would say and do if he were still by her side. She knew in her heart that he would encourage her to persevere. And so she did.

FAREWELL TO THE QUEEN

(1932)

Three months later, at seventy-three years old, with the help of leading members of the magic community, including Harry Houdini and Harry Blackstone Jr., Adelaide built a new show. She called her final production Grace, Magic, and Music. It featured her performing in pantomime with smaller-scale illusions that included color-changing handkerchiefs, disappearing doves, and a beautiful vanishing assistant. Within a few years of her return to the stage, Adelaide's health began to fail. She could no longer keep pace with

the demands of performing and touring. In 1928, the time had come to announce her retirement.

Four years later, on February 19, 1932, Adelaide died of pneumonia at the age of seventy-nine. At the funeral, she received the ultimate magician's honor for her courage and devotion to the art: the broken wand ceremony. This is a ritual where a magic wand is broken over the casket of a magician. It symbolizes the end of a magician's power.

Was it really the end, or was it the beginning? Imagine magic during its golden age without its queen leading the way. Adelaide was buried in New York's Woodlawn Cemetery next to her true love, Alexander. His gravestone was marked "Husband," with both his name and stage name, Herrmann the Great, carved underneath. Adelaide's gravestone was marked "Wife," with her name engraved below. Unlike Alexander's, Adelaide's grave made no mention of a stage name.

1841 BOSTON MUSEUM 1876

Mr. R. M. Field. Manager

Boston Museum.
(ESTABLISHED 1841.)

THE SUMMER SEASON !

WILL BE INAUGURATED

MONDAY, JULY 10th,

With a production of Messrs. Rice & Goodwin's
Famous American Opera Bouffe,

Evangeline

—WITH AN—

UNEXAMPLED

THE WONDER OF THE 19TH CENTURY !

THE GREAT AND ONLY

HERRMANN !

PREMIER OF ALL MAGICIANS !

LAST PERFORMANCES !

Saturday Afternoon and Evening, July 8, 1876.

ROGRAMME.

...ill explain how it is done.) 8, The Indian Puzzle. 9,

EGYPTIAN HALL,
PICCADILLY.

HERRMA

HAVE YOU SEEN HE
IN HIS SPLENDID SALOON

EGYPTIAN HALL, PI
IN HIS UNPARALLELED

NECROMA
DELAY NOT, BUT GO
THE PUBLIC
Are unanimous that he is a Phenom

PRESTIDIGIT
And must be Seen to be Believed, such

ACTS OF LEGER
PROFESSO

HERRM

Sold at Mitchell's Royal Library, Bond Street, and all the
Office, St. James's Hal

PRICES OF ADMISSION — Full Sofa (3 Seats) £
Fauteuils. (Reserved) 5s.
Area. 2s.
Box Office at the Egyptian Hall, open from Eleven t

Baker's Art Gallery
COLUMBUS, O.

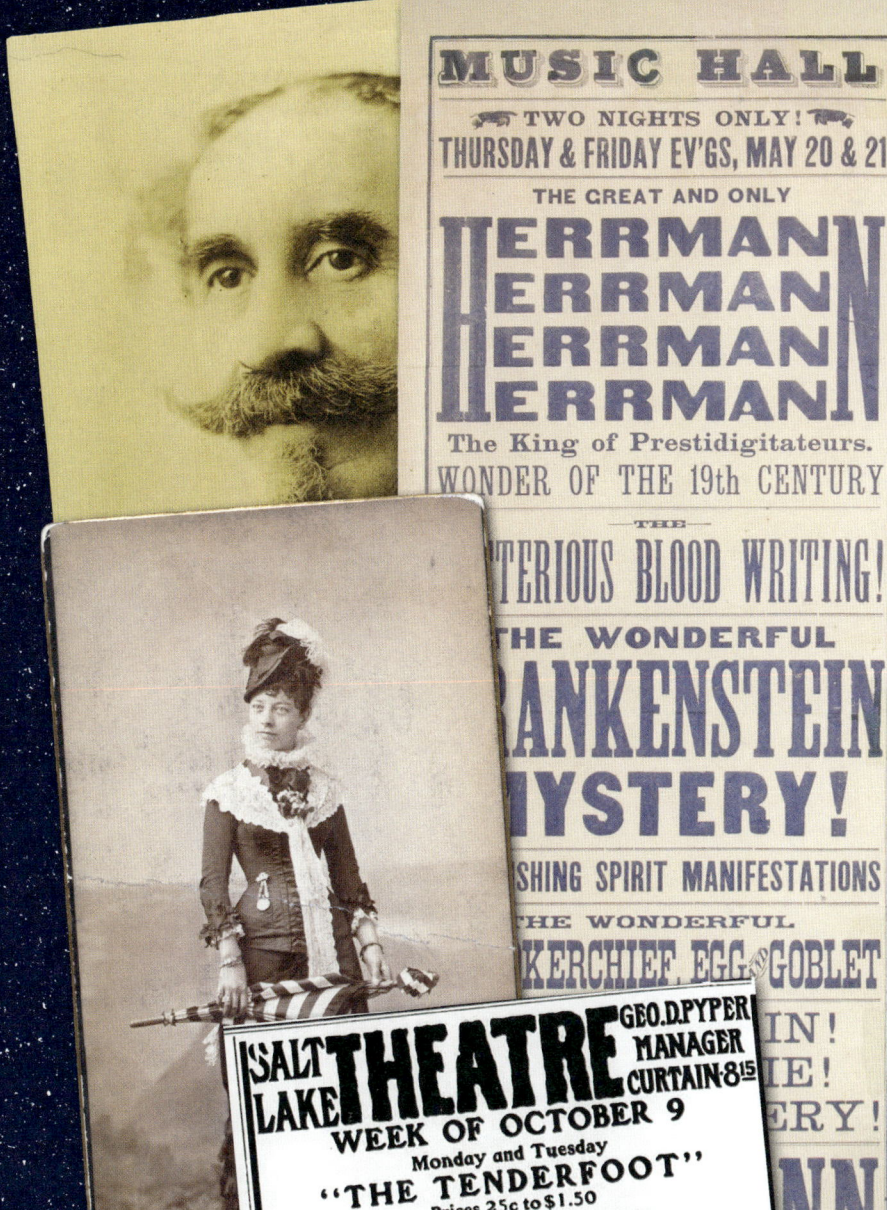

DIXIE HAYGOOD

ANNIE ABBOTT,
LITTLE GEORGIA MAGNET

THE STRONGWOMAN

DECEMBER 13, 1860–NOVEMBER 21, 1915

DIXIE'S ORIGIN STORY

1860–1886

Newspapers around the globe declared Dixie Annie Jarratt the strongest woman in the world! She weighed ninety-eight pounds. No one could predict that this mild-mannered and soft-spoken woman could over-power any man who dared to step onstage with her. She puzzled doctors and scientists and charmed nobles and celebrities with her quiet confidence and invisible power. Some called her a witch, a fake, a fraud. Others tried to imitate her, even steal her name. In the late nineteenth century, electricity was still a mystery to most Americans. Before sold-out audiences in America and abroad, Dixie displayed superhuman strength that she claimed was an electrical force at work. She captured the imagination of a generation of women whose socially acceptable roles of mother and wife did not include performing the impossible. Dixie wrote her own rulebook on what a woman could be and could do. Dixie was fearless, and like Anna Eva Fay and Adelaide Herrmann, she found a way to develop her talents despite the strict gender roles of the time. She dared to take on the world in unexpected ways.

In her own telling, Dixie first discovered her mysterious power in the small rural town of Milledgeville, Georgia. Born on December 13, 1860, she came of age during the Reconstruction Era in a poor family with few options for their children. Dixie's mother was a homemaker. Her father was a tinner who repaired household wares in their small community, barely making ends meet. In 1878, Dixie married her childhood sweetheart, Charles Haygood. The young couple, anxious to escape the ruins of the Civil War that surrounded them in their small Georgian town, set out to make a fresh start. They packed their meager belongings and moved to Waco, Texas. In 1879, Dixie gave birth to her first child. Sadly, she lost the baby within a year. When she gave birth to her second child, a girl she named Maud, the family returned home to Georgia to build a life surrounded by Dixie's extended family. Four years later, she gave birth to a boy named Fred. While Dixie cared for her two children, Charles found a steady job in Milledgeville working as a deputy marshal. At twenty-two years old, it appeared that Dixie had settled into a quiet domestic life, raising a family while her husband went to work each day.

All that changed one winter evening in 1885 when Charles took Dixie out on a date to the local theater. A teenager named Lulu Hurst, also Georgian, had come to town to exhibit her mysterious powers onstage. Lulu claimed to have been possessed by a magnetic force during an electrical thunderstorm when she was just fourteen years old. She described how lightning struck her home and loud popping sounds traveled through her entire house, followed by the smell of sulfur that seeped through the walls and floorboards. The strange sounds and smell continued for days.

Lulu explained how soon after the lightning struck, articles of clothing started disappearing from one dresser and reappearing in another dresser; a hat lifted into the air and was transported out of one room into another by an invisible force. She described other unusual goings-on outside the house, like nuts from the family's hickory tree randomly flying into the house and hitting people as they walked by an opened window. Lulu began noticing changes in herself too. She discovered that she suddenly possessed unusual strength. When her parents tested her claim, she proved remarkably strong. Finally, they declared that it was not the house that was possessed by the mysterious electrical force—it was Lulu!

Intrigued by Lulu's inexplicable new power, neighbors stopped by to witness the unusual events. They couldn't believe what they saw. Word spread about this extraordinary phenomenon. This led to great public interest, so Lulu and her father created a stage show in which Lulu tested her powers on anyone who paid to attend. Lulu traveled the country performing incredible feats of strength. By the time she and her father had arrived at the Milledgeville Opera House, they had spent two successful years on the road. In that time, Lulu achieved great wealth and international fame. The world now knew her as the Georgia Wonder!

Dixie and Charles waited in their seats with great anticipation. Finally, Lulu entered the stage to begin her performance. Lulu's father started by requesting the largest men in the audience join her onstage. Charles volunteered. Dixie watched in amazement as he, along with three other heavyset men, climbed onstage. The men's combined weight must have been well over 500 pounds. They were instructed to pile onto a single chair, one on top of the other. Lulu stood behind them with her hand barely touching the back of the chair. Once the men positioned themselves on the chair, she took a moment to channel her invisible power. Then, with the gentle touch of her open palm, she calmly tipped the chair over and sent the men flying onto the floor in all directions. The amazed audience erupted into laughter. Lulu displayed other feats of strength that night. She held a billiard cue vertically, stood on one foot, and dared the male volunteers to push her off balance. None succeeded. How could a teenage girl possess such force? Was this an inexplicable act of nature that scientists couldn't explain, or was it a magic trick?

Dixie sat in awe. She wondered what it would feel like to possess all that power in one hand. It wasn't just Lulu's show of extraordinary strength, but the casual way in which she overpowered the men that set Dixie's imagination spinning. She saw herself in this remarkable teenager and believed this spectacular illusion was within her reach.

After the show, she rushed home and stayed up for hours experimenting with ways to re-create Lulu's performance. She was possessed. Inspired! She started with a simple prop, most likely a cane, or maybe it was a billiard cue? Something close to what Lulu used onstage. Then she tested the stunt by standing on one foot while she and Charles held on to the billiard cue. She experimented with having Charles sit in a wooden chair to test how Lulu sent the men tumbling onto the stage floor. She considered the subtle ways in which Lulu positioned her body, how she held her elbows, and where she placed her hands. Since Lulu had worn a long dress, Dixie could only guess where Lulu might have positioned her feet. Were they wide apart or close together? Was one in front of the other, or were they side by side? Sometime past midnight, the secret was revealed to her. Like a vision, the mechanics of how Lulu resisted the men's force came into focus. In that moment, she also saw how she could design a future for herself beyond Milledgeville. Since she had married and started a family so young, she never had the chance to imagine beyond her own survival—until now.

Almost as quickly as Dixie uncovered the secret behind Lulu's illusion of strength, she began crafting her origin story. She knew that her actual background—a young mother with a simple life struggling to put food on the table—wouldn't sell tickets. She had to conjure a bigger, more fantastic tale. Her newly invented story began when she was just seven years old. She claimed to have suddenly discovered that she could lift her father off the floor without the least bit of exertion. In some accounts, Dixie changed her story, claiming that it was her older brother who she could lift with inexplicable ease. She further recounted that she had kept her secret power to herself until the evening she witnessed the Georgia Wonder, Lulu Hurst, exhibit the same force.

Dixie first tested her strange power in public for small gatherings of friends and neighbors. Encouraged by the positive response, Charles helped her land bookings at nearby community halls and on small stages while Dixie continued to fine-tune the illusion. For her act, she wore long, flowing dresses covered with ruffles. She spoke softly to create the impression of a delicate woman and to contrast with the hefty men she selected to challenge her onstage. She played up the frail and helpless image by stepping on a scale at the start of each show to prove her ninety-eight-pound weight. To win over journalists in each town, Dixie gave private performances in advance of her shows. The goal was to shut down any potential skeptics. Before showtime, she and Charles researched the crowd so they knew exactly who to select to join Dixie onstage. Charles made sure to choose the most respected citizens in each town to witness her magnetic force. If esteemed townspeople believed Dixie's mysterious power, then the rest of the audience would too.

In 1885, the same year she began performing in public, Dixie's father passed away. A year later, Dixie gave birth to another son, Charles Jr. With a growing family, she began to rely more on her mother to care for her young children while she established herself as a stage magician. Charles, meanwhile, held down his deputy job by day and hustled bookings as Dixie's manager by night. He proved to be an ideal partner for her. Together, they shared the dream of breaking out of their small town to try their luck at a better life. Dixie's act would be their ticket to a new world. Then, just as Dixie's act was building momentum with Charles at her side, a local bootlegger and anti-prohibitionist shot and killed Charles while he was on duty. The murder sent Dixie into a tailspin. To add to her pain, the killer walked free.

PRESENTING THE LITTLE GEORGIA MAGNET
(1886—1889)

At twenty-four years old, with three young children to care for, Dixie's illusion-making was her only means of income. She had to teach herself how to launch and manage a career as a solo woman magician in order to survive. Three years after Charles's death, Dixie re-emerged, this time with a new name and a new manager. During her absence, she had evidently married a younger man who had abandoned her and left her penniless. Journalists caught wind of the controversy and followed the story, publishing updates in the gossip sections of local newspapers. Was this all part of Dixie's strategy to promote ticket sales before her return to the stage? Or was there some truth to her woeful tale of a hasty and failed marriage to a cad who ran off with her earnings and all her belongings?

Dixie's new manager, Richard Abbey, soon became her third husband. Similar to Henry Melville's role in Anna Eva Fay's early career, Richard brought stage and business experience to the partnership. He helped build on the invented mythology of how Dixie came to be possessed by this mysterious and powerful force. He spun her act into new directions, bringing more attention and regular bookings in the emerging vaudeville circuit that included magic acts as part of its eclectic repertoire. Reborn now as Annie Abbott, the Little Georgia Magnet, Dixie had reimagined Lulu's act with a few personal twists. Lulu never challenged Dixie for "borrowing" her act, since by the time Dixie had reinvented herself as Annie Abbott, Lulu had retired from public life. Perfect timing for a new electric girl to take over the spotlight!

Dixie, the Original Annie Abbott, continued to advance her shows with private press-only previews, but that wasn't enough to stay competitive since other

"electric girls" had sprung up, claiming the same mysterious power. Dixie needed something eye-catching, newsworthy, sensational. During this time, scientists had taken an interest in her powers. Dr. Lewis Pedigo, a Virginian doctor and member of the American Society of Psychical Research, invited Dixie to be hypnotized so he could test her abilities while under a trance. Dixie had asserted that the only time her powers were weakened was if she stood on a carpeted floor. For some reason, the conductivity of her electric force could only travel through a wood floor or through glass. Dr. Pedigo decided to test her strength both on and off a carpet while she fell into a deep sleep and was allegedly unaware of her surroundings. Just as Anna Eva Fay's mind-reading powers had been tested by scientist William Crookes, Dixie partook in a controlled, "scientific" experiment to test her extraordinary strength.

Under Dr. Pedigo's close observation, Dixie successfully performed her feats of strength while standing on a wooden floor. When the doctor tested her strength on a woolen carpet, her powers ceased to exist. His conclusion: Dixie possessed a new kind of magnetic force he called nerve force. Could this have been a publicity stunt, or was Dixie truly baffling the scientific minds of her day? This finding by an "expert" delighted Dixie and Richard. They used the endorsement to add to Dixie's credibility and expand their tour. Whether it was staged or authentic, the public believed it and it worked to fill seats.

As part of their publicity campaign, Dixie carefully avoided referring to her act as magic, instead calling her illusions "experiments." In many ways, science in the late nineteenth century was a form of magic to most Americans. The inventions that would transform the world, such as the telephone, phonograph, automobile, motion picture camera, and the lightbulb, still held great mystery to the general public. Dixie's act capitalized on this innovation in science and technology by creating the illusion that humans could possess electrical power. She even claimed that inventor Thomas Edison himself confirmed that she possessed a power that could only be explained as electrical force.

A SERIES OF ENTERTAINMENTS

(1889—1891)

Within the first year of Dixie's debut as Annie Abbott, she had become a regular in vaudeville. The audiences welcomed Dixie's strongwoman act. Her exceptional skill paved the way for the successful beginning of her young career. She cleverly stayed in the public's eye with newsworthy stunts that she staged around her engagements. While on tour in California, she invited a group of women volunteers from the audience to investigate her by bathing her backstage before her performance. Dixie wanted to prove that she wore no devices under her clothing that could aid in her remarkable feats. The stunt drew big headlines and attracted a full house! Dixie continued to create the illusion of possessing extra-human strength by enlisting a doctor to take her temperature onstage before each show. Her temperature invariably measured ten degrees below normal. This sent a message to the crowd that there was something unusual about Dixie's physical state. It built intrigue and suspense before the curtain even rose.

While on tour, Dixie also expanded her origin story. In one interview, she recounted how she was struck by lightning three times as a child. Her teeth were so charged with electricity that metal objects were attracted to them. These outrageous claims drew even more crowds. Dixie's star was rising. With the help of Richard's shrewd management and clever promotional skills, the two set out on a cross-country tour of sold-out bookings. The Little Georgia Magnet was becoming a star!

A typical evening began with Richard entering the stage and introducing the one and only Original Annie Abbott, the Little Georgia Magnet! He would then describe the mystery surrounding this gentle, ninety-eight pound woman, who could miraculously overpower the strongest men in the world!

One of the most popular feats of strength Dixie performed was the **Chair Test**.

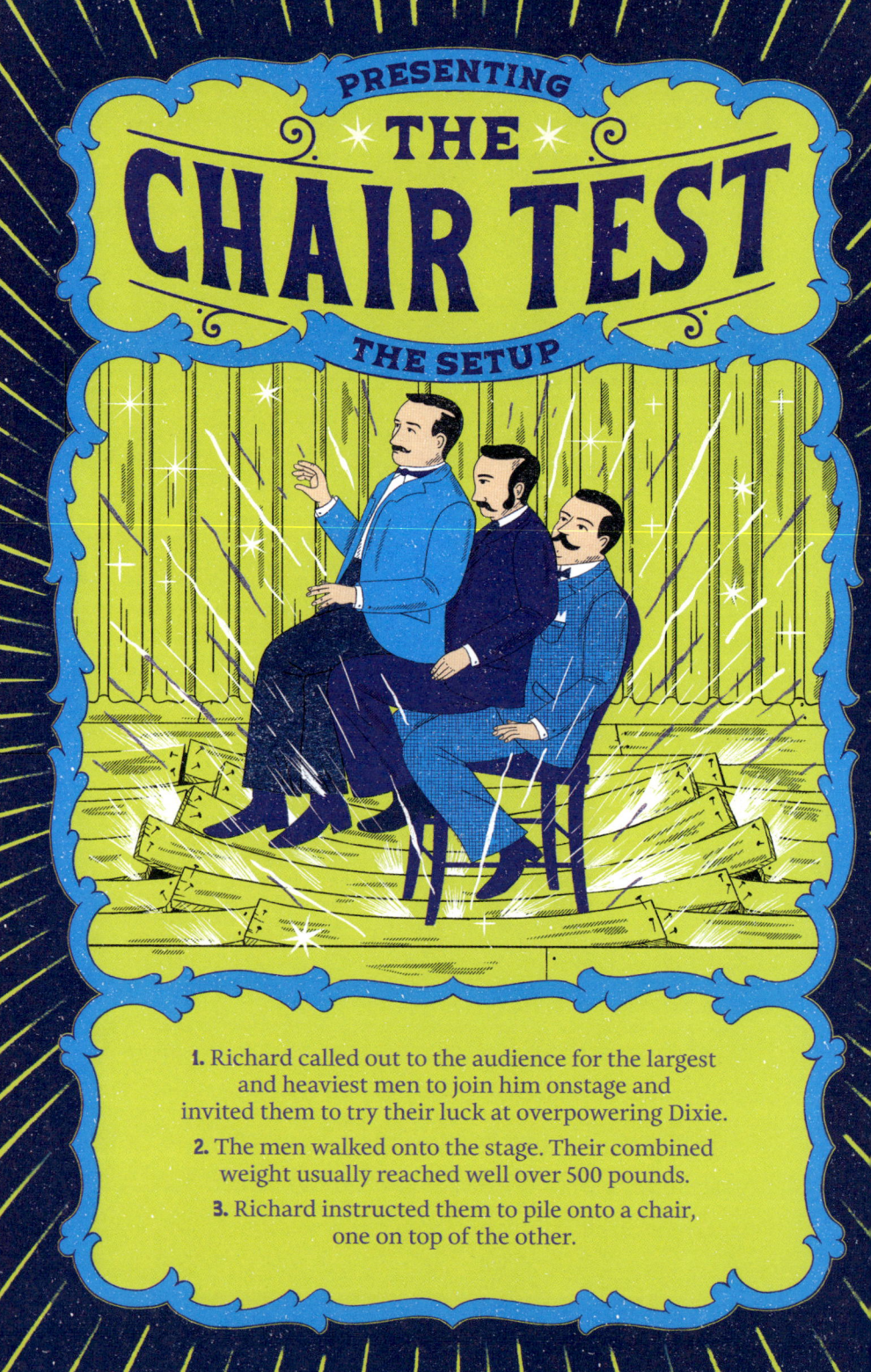

THE CHAIR TEST

THE REVEAL

1. With a sly smile, Dixie quietly observed the men balancing on one another on the chair.

2. Dixie closed her eyes, took a long pause, and channeled the electric force from deep inside.

3. She lightly touched the back of the chair with her open palm.

4. Suddenly, the men lifted off the chair and tumbled onto the floor in all directions.

For another illusion, Richard invited an audience member to press a drinking glass against Dixie's skin. The volunteer reported hearing a strange buzzing sound vibrating from the glass that could only be explained as an electrical current running through her body.

A further test featured Dixie holding a wooden billiard cue vertically and challenging a handful of the strongest men in the audience to try to move her from her standing position.

PRESENTING
THE
BILLIARD CUE
TEST

THE SETUP

1. Dixie held up a wooden billiard cue.

2. Once again, Richard requested male volunteers.

3. A handful of men from the audience stepped onto the stage.

4. He then instructed them to hold on to the billiard cue tightly.

THE BILLIARD CUE TEST

THE REVEAL

1. Dixie lifted one foot off the ground and balanced on the other.

2. With a delicate touch, she placed her open palm against the billiard cue that the men were holding on to.

3. The male volunteers tried with all their strength to move her from her fixed position but failed.

4. Some of the men also said they felt an electrical vibration passing through their bodies, and were convinced that this caused them to lose all strength.

Dixie's act challenged the conventional wisdom of the time that women were expected to stay at home and take on domestic duties, not flaunt their power over men in public and earn an income doing it!

As Dixie's children grew older, she included them in her performances. She planted them in her audiences on occasion and selected them as volunteers to help her with her act. For one illusion, Dixie trained her son Fred, who was now five years old, to hold out a silk handkerchief to her. She pretended to send an electrical force through the handkerchief. She then called on volunteers from the audience to attempt to move young Fred from his fixed position. Each time, they failed. It appeared that Dixie could not only control her own electrical force, but also create the illusion of transferring her power to another person. It was a new stunt that intrigued and baffled audiences.

With Dixie's growing fame and popularity, she began to mix with notable figures of the day, including boxing legends John L. Sullivan and Jake Kilrain. They professed to be the strongest men in the world, that is until they stepped onstage to challenge Dixie. She overpowered both of them and showed them otherwise! It didn't take long for skeptics to emerge. They published various theories debunking Dixie's strange power. Dixie paid little mind to the doubters since it was all part of the hazards of illusion-making. Creating the image of an unstoppable strongwoman was her only means of survival. She couldn't concede to her critics. She needed to keep moving.

KINGS, QUEENS, AND DIAMONDS

(1891—1893)

In 1891, Richard and Dixie, along with Dixie's youngest son, Charlie, boarded a passenger steamer headed to England. She left her two other children, Maud and Fred, under the care of her mother in Milledgeville. Dixie decided to take the trip across the Atlantic in hopes of conjuring more positive press and escaping the mounting exposers, just as Anna Eva Fay had done to elude her skeptics. With new income and advance bookings at one of the most popular venues in London, the Alhambra Theatre, Dixie played up her growing success on the American stage to a new audience of potential patrons on the ocean steamer. During the Atlantic crossing, she strolled around the ship wrapped in a mink coat, flashing diamond necklaces, gold bracelets, and sparkling pins to give the appearance of wealth and sophistication. In truth, she was barely scraping by. While on the voyage, Dixie also performed paid private shows for rich passengers who she charmed into becoming her biggest fans. She even claimed that she used her invisible force to propel the engine toward England's rocky shores faster than scheduled. The favorable word of mouth that resulted was just what she needed before setting foot in a new country where she was still untested.

Before Dixie's European debut, she performed for the Prince of Wales at Sandringham, the royal family's country home. After that performance, she befriended the future king of England and spent time with him. On one of her visits, she claimed to have cured him of a migraine with her special powers. Her entry into the world of the well-connected suited her. She was living a fairy-tale dream that she never could have imagined as a young girl growing up in rural Georgia.

Finally, the night had come to perform at Alhambra Theatre in Leicester Square. Little Dixie Haygood, who now billed herself as Annie Abbott, the Little Georgia Wonder, was about to walk onto one of the most popular stages in London to perform for a capacity crowd of over 2,000 spectators. Her first performance on November 16, 1891, was extremely well received. The mysterious force she possessed brought great excitement to audiences. The following day, she received glowing

CASINO DE PARIS

TOUS LES SOIRS

ANNIE ABBOTT

L'INEXPLICABLE MYSTÈRE

Lith. F. APPEL 12 R. DE DELTA PARIS

reviews. The positive publicity led to more packed houses during the run. But things took a turn when a journalist from one of London's evening newspapers, *The Star*, published exactly how Dixie created her illusion of strength. The lengthy article detailed the simple physics of the trick. It showed how Dixie held her body and positioned her elbows and feet to prevent herself from being lifted. The illusion was exposed!

Dixie refused to allow *The Star* controversy to overshadow her debut European tour. A conjurer's skills must include misdirection, the technique of distracting the audience from how the trick is actually performed. After losing some credibility in London circles, Dixie switched her plans and set up bookings away from England at venues in France, Germany, Austria, Italy, Poland, and even Russia, where she was received by enthusiastic audiences.

NO PLACE LIKE HOME
(1893—1894)

In September 1893, after almost three years of touring and performing abroad, Dixie and Richard finally returned home. Once Dixie landed on American soil, she traveled straight to Milledgeville to reunite with her family, while Richard stayed in New York to set up bookings for their next tour. Dixie had not seen her two younger children since she had first set sail for England. After spending time with her family and resting, she was ready to get back to performing. It was then that she uncovered a terrible secret. Richard had deceived her. Instead of setting up their upcoming American return to the stage, he had spent all their European earnings courting another woman and had run off with her. To further the betrayal, he trained his love interest to become the newest Annie Abbott. The only difference in this copycat act was that he added the middle name May to the advertisements and bookings. Otherwise, it was the same act that had launched Dixie's successful career. And Richard moved quickly to set up a rival tour, leaving Dixie to fend for herself.

With the steady determination that had brought Dixie this far, she returned to performing on her own. To separate herself from Annie *May* Abbott, she added a more daring stunt called the **Battering Ram** to her show.

PRESENTING
THE
BATTERING RAM
THE SETUP

1. Dixie requested a dozen (or sometimes more) men to join her onstage.

2. She asked for them to stand in a straight line with one arm holding the shirt collar of the man in front of him. Imagine a line of human dominos.

THE ✦ BATTERING RAM

THE REVEAL

1. Dixie stood at the front of the line and applied her mysterious force as the men pushed forward trying to force her off-balance.

2. Miraculously, she appeared unaffected by their combined strength. Instead of losing her balance, the reverse happened. Each of the burly men fell backward, tumbling onto the floor.

3. The illusion of a petite woman overpowering over a dozen hefty men left the audience thoroughly entertained!

Despite Dixie's ability to persevere and set up new bookings across the country, she privately struggled. Supporting her children with only the help of her aging mother proved to be a challenge. Around this time, Dixie began complaining of severe headaches and fatigue. Although she claimed she possessed her own healing powers through her mysterious electric force, she was unable heal herself. She even offered a reward of $10,000 to anyone who could cure her of the mystifying illness. Was this a show-woman's stunt to draw attention to her performances? Or had the travel, exposures, imitators, and Richard's betrayal taken a toll on Dixie's mental and physical health?

THE SECRET EXPOSED!

(1894)

In the fall of 1894, Dixie brought her strongwoman act to New York City. Her first stop was the celebrated *New York World*, one of the largest newspapers of the time, known for its eye-catching headlines and human-interest stories. The newspaper had a circulation of over 300,000. Before her visit, the paper had staged a publicity stunt where Dixie took on German-born Eugen Sandow, one the strongest men in the world. When he fell

to Dixie's extraordinary power, he wrote a public letter to the editor of *The New York World* assuring the readers of Dixie's authenticity and phenomenal strength.

Two days later, Dixie stopped by the *New York World* office to preview her act to a roomful of journalists with the goal of charming them into publishing favorable reviews before her upcoming New York engagement. While a dozen male journalists watched in awe as Dixie overpowered the strongest men in the room, the only female journalist present that day sat quietly in the back with a keen eye on Dixie's every move. Her name was Elizabeth Jane Cochrane, better known as Nellie Bly. Only a few years earlier, Nellie had gone undercover, posing as a patient to expose the inhumane treatment of the mentally ill. Nellie was a fierce and passionate investigative journalist who sought out the truth and injustices wherever she found them. On this particular New York City afternoon, she closely observed Dixie as she wowed the small crowd of news writers with her display of electrical force. Nellie was not convinced. From the start, she doubted the alleged power. She carefully searched for clues. She noted that Dixie was a petite woman with blond hair and piercing blue eyes who on that day wore a plaid silk lavender dress with ruffles at the neck. She observed the jewelry that adorned Dixie. The diamond pin, a belt of silver coins, the gemmed rings on her fingers, and the gold bracelets on her delicate wrists. She deduced that these jewels were likely gifts from royalty given to Dixie during her famed European tour just a few years earlier. Still, Nellie was not impressed.

After Dixie's demonstration, Nellie got straight to work. She leaped from her chair and began her line of questioning. She first asked why Dixie needed a wooden floor to access the force. Why was it that she couldn't access the same force while standing on a woolen carpet? Instead of responding, Dixie began recounting her origin story to switch the focus. She claimed that when she was a little girl, her brother had tried to lift her, but she had somehow found a way to make herself heavy. She asserted that scientists were baffled by her strange force and could not agree on an explanation for it. Nellie had a hunch there was more to the story than what Dixie was revealing. She decided to volunteer to test Dixie's strength firsthand. Dixie resisted at first, sensing that Nellie was out to expose her. Nellie persisted. With the other *New York World* journalists in attendance, Dixie had no other choice than to accept Nellie's challenge.

Dixie placed her hand on Nellie's back and neck and positioned another male editor's hands beneath Nellie's arms. Dixie then closed her eyes and sent her magnetic force through the editor's hands to Nellie. When the male editor tried to lift Nellie off the floor, he failed. Nellie was still unconvinced. At that moment, a young office worker walked into the room to deliver a telegram. Nellie challenged Dixie to test the young man on the spot, and Dixie agreed. She placed her left hand on the young office worker's hand and her right hand on his back. When a group of male editors tried to lift the young boy off the floor, they failed. That's when Nellie spotted a clue! She saw that Dixie had pressed down on the back and wrist of the office worker as the men pushed upward. The male volunteers who attempted to move the young worker from his fixed position were using their own force against themselves! When Nellie confronted Dixie about her observation, Dixie quickly excused herself, feigning a migraine. She quietly slipped out of *The New York World*'s newspaper offices and onto the busy street outside, disappearing into the crowd.

Once Dixie had left the building, Nellie performed the stunt with her male colleagues. None of them could move her, proving that no mysterious force was ever present with Dixie. It was simple physics. A magic trick! Within a few days, Nellie published the entire story, exposing exactly how Dixie performed her alleged feat of superhuman strength. She boasted in a *New York World* headline "Bly Is a Magnet, Too." Dixie refused to let the negative publicity stop her. She stepped right back onstage, just as she had done in England after *The Star* attacked her credibility. A week later, a notice in *The New York World*'s evening edition on October 5, 1894, advertised that Annie Abbott, the Little Georgia Magnet, was performing at New York City's Koster and Bial's Music Hall, for 50 cents admission. The show must go on, and it did!

THE LAST HURRAH

(1895—1915)

For the next fifteen years, Dixie toured the country playing to packed houses. Behind the scenes, her challenges mounted. She not only had to evade increasing numbers of detractors, but her nemesis, Annie *May* Abbott, was circling the country with Richard pulling the strings. Annie May Abbott performed Dixie's mystifying magnetism act, creating confusion among booking

agents and audiences. They wondered who the original Annie Abbott was. Dixie made several attempts to control her public image by publishing warnings in local newspapers about the deception whenever and wherever she knew the couple would be appearing. But it failed to stop Annie May Abbott and Richard's highly publicized cross-country and international engagements. One night in Chicago, after a performance, Dixie stepped offstage and was greeted by two policemen, who promptly handcuffed her. They insisted that she had bought diamonds at a nearby Chicago jewelry store but had never paid the bill. Thinking quickly, Dixie insisted that they were mistaken, saying they must have been looking for the other Annie Abbott, Annie May Abbott, who was traveling with her ex-husband. The policemen apologized for the inconvenience and promptly uncuffed her. Dixie might not have been able to stop her imitators, but she certainly could slow them down!

Although Dixie had achieved much success as a performer, her turbulent personal life was ultimately her undoing. Her older children became estranged from her. She married twice more. Each of the marriages were short-lived. Extended family members took the responsibility of caring for her children as Dixie's mental state began to decline. Then, in 1901, Dixie lost her son Charley to heart disease. He had traveled with her on her famed European tour at the peak of her career and was one of the few children who remained devoted to her. This loss devastated her. She never truly recovered.

Eventually, the excitement of travel and the applause of adoring crowds began to lose its appeal. Dixie's star was fading as more Annie Abbotts sprung up around her, asserting the same mysterious power that had brought her notoriety. Her complaints of headaches and a mystery illness that no doctor could cure escalated. With both Dixie's physical and mental health failing, she retreated to her hometown of Milledgeville, seeking refuge at her family home. She lived alone there, isolated from the world that she had once sought to conquer.

On November 21, 1915, at just fifty-four years old, she quietly passed away and was buried in an unmarked grave. After the magic that she conjured for admirers from around the globe and after an incredible journey as a woman who forged her own path when most women wouldn't dare, Dixie Haygood, the Original Annie Abbott, just disappeared.

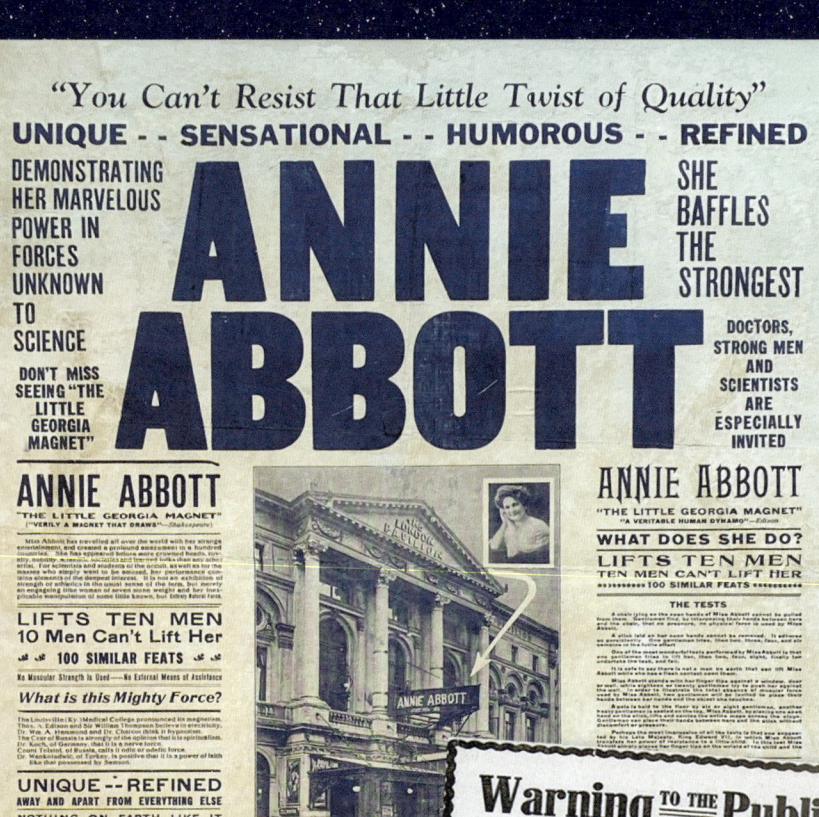

EXTRA!
ADDED ATTRACTION
'The Little Georgia Magnet'
ANNIE ABBOT
"A VERITABLE HUMAN DYNAMO"
according to
Thomas A. Edison.
Other scientists also baffled.

Her
extraordinary performance
is

- Unique - Refined

SEE WHAT SHE DOES

"Make the coming o'erflow with joy
And pleasure drown the brim.
—*Shakespeare.*

KOSTER & BIALS.

KOSTER & BIAL.

s of Force Easy,
World Woman Writer

3

Lansberg, Student of
Witchcraft and Mechanical Tricks, She Per-
forms the Stunts of Annie Abbott, "Georgia
Magnet," Which Have Mystified Scientists.

By Grace Nicholas.

had placed my fingers. As the man

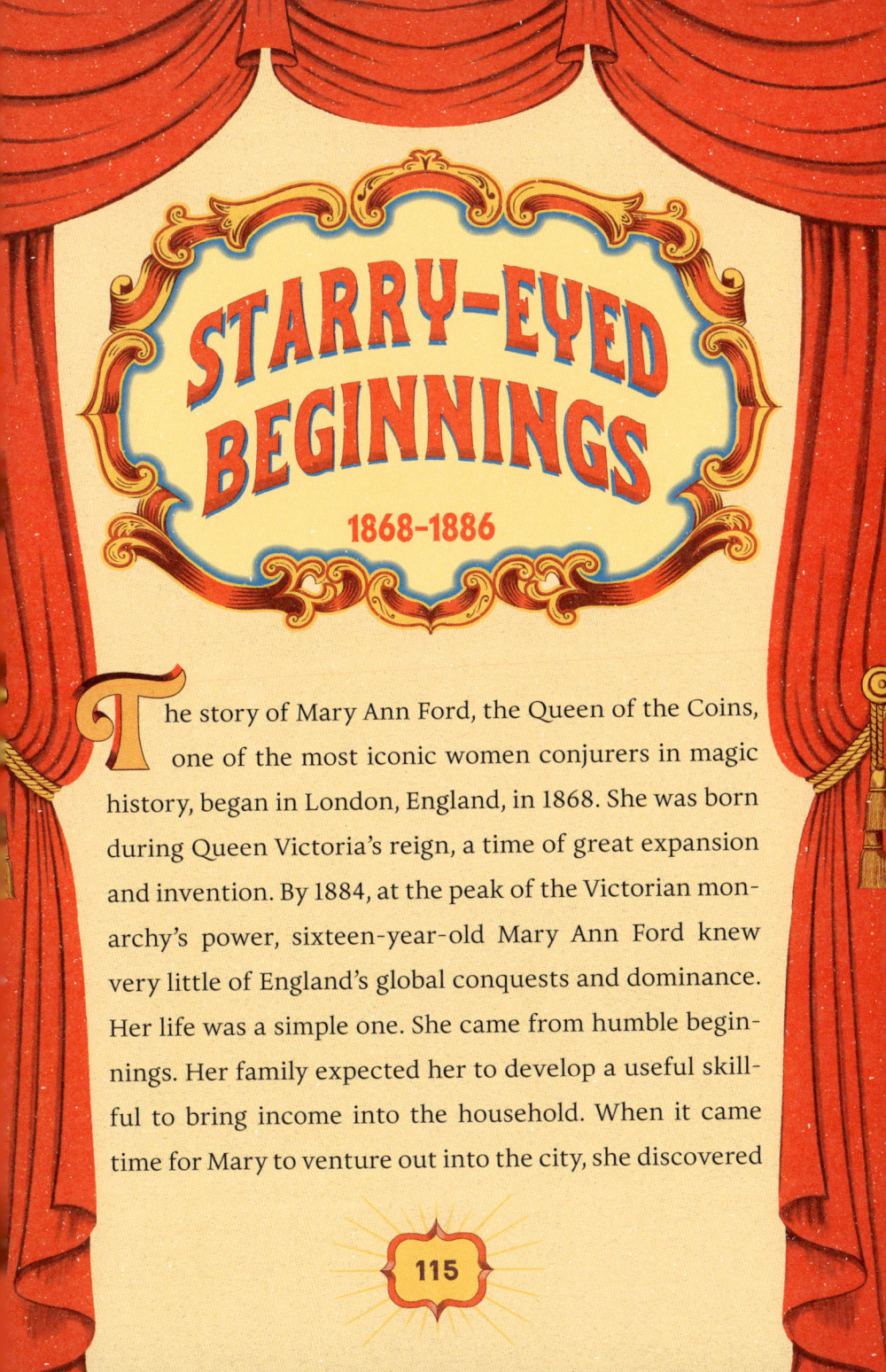

STARRY-EYED BEGINNINGS

1868-1886

The story of Mary Ann Ford, the Queen of the Coins, one of the most iconic women conjurers in magic history, began in London, England, in 1868. She was born during Queen Victoria's reign, a time of great expansion and invention. By 1884, at the peak of the Victorian monarchy's power, sixteen-year-old Mary Ann Ford knew very little of England's global conquests and dominance. Her life was a simple one. She came from humble beginnings. Her family expected her to develop a useful skillful to bring income into the household. When it came time for Mary to venture out into the city, she discovered an opportunity that intrigued and inspired her—the theater!

Mary began as an observer, watching the wonderment from afar. She sat in the front row soaking in all the varieties of entertainment in London at the time—marionettes dancing on strings, trained elephants playing trumpets, trapeze artists flying through the air, and dogs performing tricks on command. Everything about this world of make-believe and spectacle delighted her. Her desire to learn more about the theater soon landed her a job as an assistant to a woman mind reader and snake charmer. Between acts, she watched the other performers in awe, absorbing all she could about how they charmed the audience with their skills and talents. She made a pact with herself right then and there that this would be her future! Mary Ann Ford from London, England, would dedicate herself to a life in the theater!

FATE INTERVENES

(1886—1890)

One evening, at a popular London venue called the Royal Aquarium, a rising star magician from Belgium named Jean Henri Servais Leroy arrived backstage. Mary had seen him perform before and had admired him from a distance. On this evening, she noted his stylish dress and larger-than-life theatrical presence. She studied how he walked and moved, the tilt of his head, the raise of his eyebrow, how he commanded a room, and the deliberate way in which he carried himself. *Like royalty*, she thought. Servais made an impression.

Servais, born in 1865 in Spa, Belgium, had a colorful childhood. He ran away from home as a young boy to live with his adopted uncle in England. Together, they moved from town to town, never settling into a permanent home. As a ten-year-old, he made an income as a horse doctor in the countryside, a skill he acquired from reading a book on the subject. He then took up soccer, which he excelled at, and earned a spot on an elite traveling soccer club. While in Wales, he met an eccentric retired naval officer who introduced him to magic. Captain Henry Worsley Hill taught young Servais the classic close-up trick known as Cups and Balls, which involves three cups and a ball that invisibly jumps from one cup to another and then *magically* multiplies into several balls.

That evening at the Royal Aquarium, Servais learned that one of his assistants had failed to show up for the performance. While pacing back and forth trying to solve his dilemma, he spotted Mary. Her blue-eyed beauty and slight frame perfectly fit the role. He approached her and explained his predicament. Mary jumped at the chance. As the audience filled the hall, Servais quickly instructed Mary on the illusion. It was a dream come true!

The red velvet curtain lifted. The music began to play. Mary watched excitedly from the wings as Servais entered the stage in a long overcoat, wearing a high silk hat, carrying a cane, and smoking a cigar. Before she could blink, the cigar and the cane had disappeared. In another moment, the top hat vanished too. Servais then tossed off his overcoat and his trousers dropped to the floor revealing knee-length britches to the amusement of the audience! He continued his quick-change magic, and in a flash, he was suddenly wearing a new velvet coat. A quick-change illusion is when a magician switches from one costume to another undetected and within seconds. Servais twirled his long, waxed mustache and stroked his pointed goatee. He had inexplicably transformed into the Devil in Evening Dress right in front of the audience's eyes!

Mary was so entranced by Servais's opening act that she forgot about her own performance. She rushed to her dressing room to prepare for her debut in an illusion called the **Three Graces**.

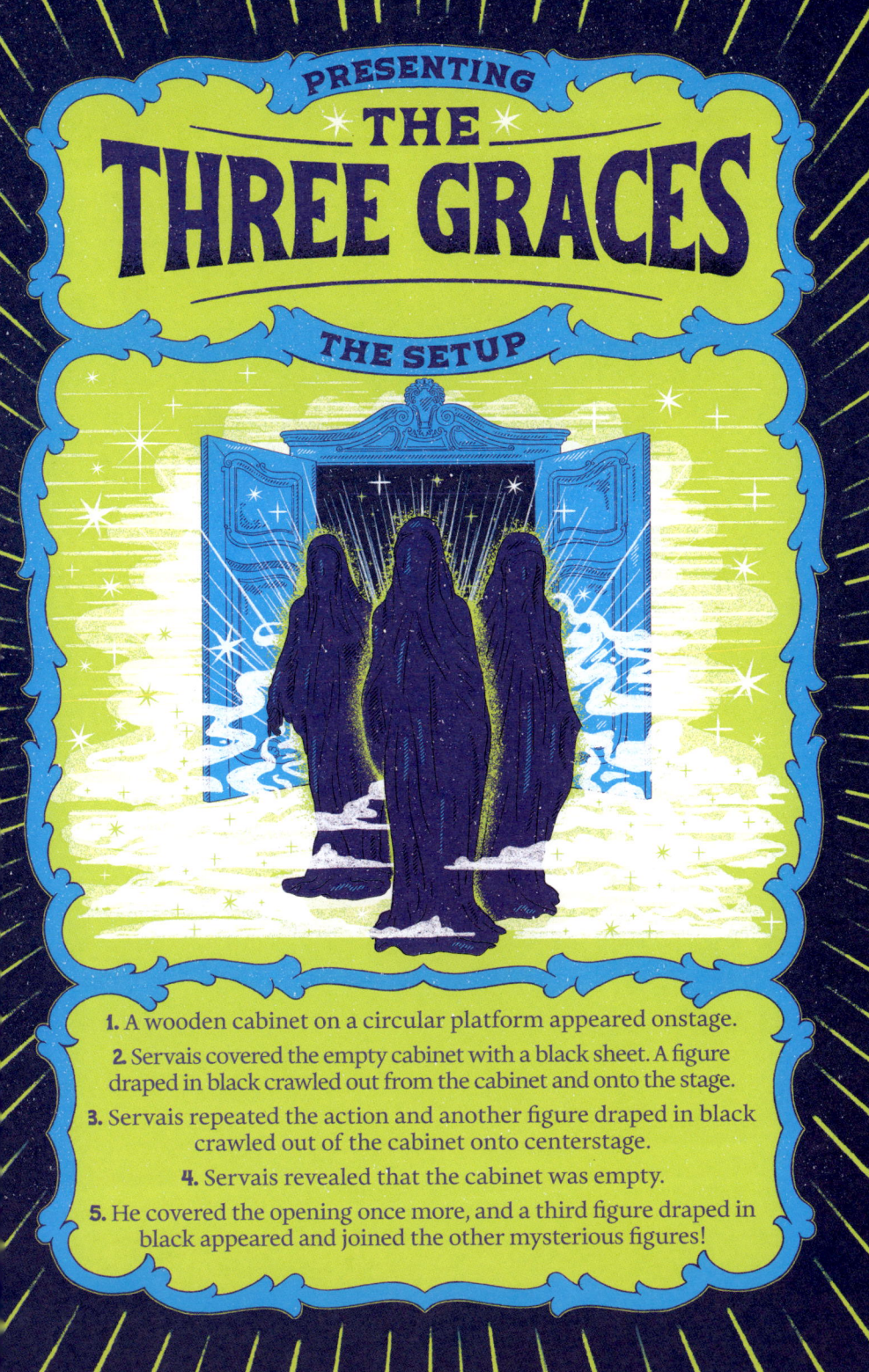

PRESENTING

THE THREE GRACES

THE SETUP

1. A wooden cabinet on a circular platform appeared onstage.

2. Servais covered the empty cabinet with a black sheet. A figure draped in black crawled out from the cabinet and onto the stage.

3. Servais repeated the action and another figure draped in black crawled out of the cabinet onto centerstage.

4. Servais revealed that the cabinet was empty.

5. He covered the opening once more, and a third figure draped in black appeared and joined the other mysterious figures!

THE THREE GRACES

THE REVEAL

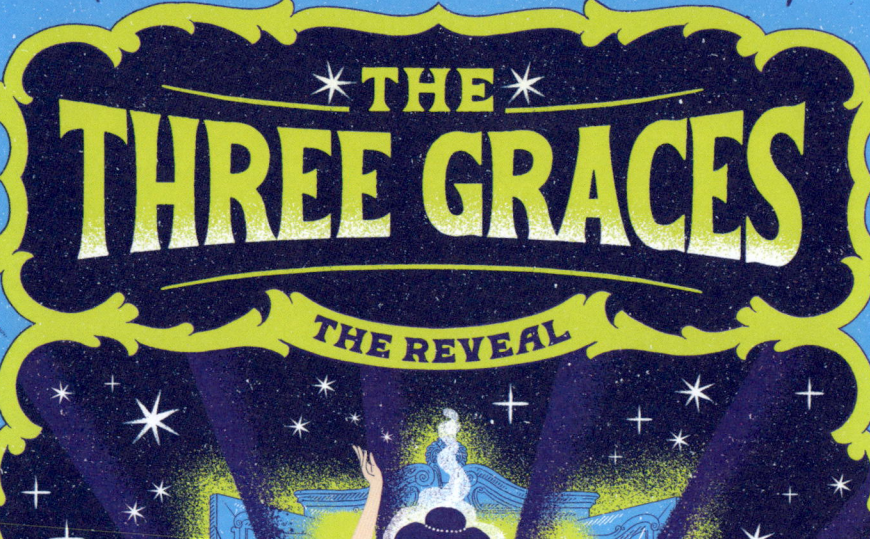

1. Servais faced the three draped figures and raised his arms.

2. He cried out, "Appear!"

3. The draped figures threw off their black cloth coverings to reveal three beautiful women. One of them was Mary Ann Ford!

4. Servais announced, "Ladies and gentlemen, the Three Graces!"

After the show, Servais invited Mary to join the troupe! Servais wasted no time in training her for the act. Once she proved herself a capable assistant for illusions beyond the Three Graces, she joined the show on a nightly basis. Servais suggested that she change her name to Mercedes Talma. Eventually, her stage name became just Talma.

Under Servais's tutorship, Talma first learned how to perform as a box jumper. A box jumper creates the illusion of disappearing from one location only to reappear in another. The role required speed, athleticism, concentration, and flair. Talma proved to possess all that, and a natural instinct for the stage. When she wasn't onstage, she studied Servais's nightly performances, taking notes. She saw the ease with which he performed his sleight of hand tricks—the skillful way in which he manipulated cards and pulled silver and gold coins out of thin air fascinated her. She wondered if she too would someday step into the spotlight as a headlining stage magician.

THE GROUNDBREAKER
(1891—1899)

In 1890, Talma became more than Servais's assistant. She married him! They recognized a shared passion for performing magic, both living for the thrill of traveling the world and performing the impossible in front of captivated audiences. Talma had emerged as a talented assistant. She became a featured player in Servais's act. As a woman working in theater without children or a home to manage, she defied the conventions of the times. Just as Anna Eva Fay, Adelaide Herrmann, and Dixie Haygood had done, Talma charted her own destiny. At twenty-two years old, she had not only found her true love, but her true calling in the world of magic!

She continued to assist Servais, but over time, she longed to step into the spotlight as a solo artist. Servais recognized her desire and agreed to teach her his arsenal of sleight of hand tricks. He spent hours training Talma and sharing his closely held trade secrets with her. She proved once again to be an apt and eager pupil. She learned how to palm coins, hide billiard balls, and produce eggs out of nowhere! Under Servais's guidance, Talma practiced tirelessly by day while working as his assistant by night.

Magicians usually have one signature trick that defines them. Talma discovered that she could palm as many as thirty half-crown coins at a time in one hand. Palming is a magician's technique for concealing objects in the palm of one's hands without the audience noticing. An English half-crown coin measured an inch and a half in diameter. Considering that Talma's hand size was a petite five and a half inches, her palming skills were extraordinary. Talma decided that coin magic would be her main attraction. She promoted herself as the Queen of Coins! In April 1899, a few months before Talma's planned debut, another coin magician named Tommy Nelson Downs stepped onto the stage at London's Palace Theatre. He gained popularity with his exceptional coin manipulation act and crowned himself the King of Koins. That didn't faze Talma. She knew she possessed a unique act that rivaled any man's, even that of the King of Koins!

On August 28, 1899, Talma stepped onstage to make her solo debut at the Oxford Theatre of Varieties.

INTRODUCING THE QUEEN OF COINS . . . TALMA!

Talma waltzed onstage against a backdrop of red plush curtains. She dressed in a long black velvet sleeveless gown with a large red rose splashed across the side. To open the act, she sang and danced, moving gracefully about the stage. She plucked gold and silver coins from the air, then dropped each coin down the clear

glass panels of the crystal ladder. The sounds of the coins traveling down the ladder added to the magical effect. She then stepped out into the audience to borrow a hat. With a flourish, she again pulled coins out of thin air, dropping them one by one into the hat. Next, strolling through more rows of spectators, she produced coins from behind the ears of one audience member after the other. To add to the illusion, she tossed a few coins high into the air, caught them, then tossed them back up in the air until the gold and silver pieces created the illusion of a shimmering shower of gold and silver. Talma playfully fooled her audience with her dexterity and speed as she kept the coins in constant motion, making a half dozen pieces appear as if they were hundreds.

Once, while on a street in New York City during a tour, she was approached by two men who attempted to rob her. She reacted quickly, producing coins out of the air and making them appear and reappear, stopping the criminals in their tracks. They were convinced Talma was a witch and fled the scene. A testament to Talma's clever performance skills!

Talma's sleight of hand technique set her apart from her male rivals. The elegant sleeveless dress she wore during her performances was a subtle nod at her male counterparts and an assurance to her audience that she had nothing up her sleeves! Her auspicious debut sparked great interest and excitement. She soon became a regular on the touring circuit in Europe. During her run at the Oxford Theatre in London, Queen Victoria's son Prince Edward insisted that his secretary contact Talma to perform for him at a private party. Word of mouth about this young woman magician sensation spread through the upper circles of London society. Talma had broken ground as a one-of-a-kind headlining female magician!

THE WORLD'S MONARCHS OF MAGIC

(1901—1930)

Talma toured her act, garnering rave reviews and establishing herself both in Europe and in America as a top sleight of hand magician. Even with her unprecedented success as a solo palm artist, Talma grew weary of performing without her beloved Servais at her side. Living on the road with a suitcase of props and a single wardrobe trunk made her lonely for the bigger illusions she had once performed with him. Talma missed the larger-scale productions, the kind of theater experience that had originally inspired her when she was that starry-eyed girl growing up in London dreaming of a life in the theater.

She was ready for something new, and so was Servais. By 1901, Servais had disbanded his trio act called The Triple Alliance. He wanted his next show to have a new twist. His idea was to create a three-ring circus of magic with Talma and a new comic magician he had discovered named Leon Bosco. They called the act LeRoy, Talma and Bosco. It was also known as The Comedians de Mephisto Co.

The show created a sensation for more than its two hours of nonstop entertainment, skillful magic, and irreverent humor. Its advertising posters featured two male magicians and a woman magician with equal billing! The trio highlighted Talma's skillful solo act alongside the best of Servais's grander illusions. Bosco provided comic interludes with a sprinkling of his own magic. Over time, there were several Boscos who took on the comic role in the troupe, but Talma and Servais spent the rest of their career performing together in this unique and popular production.

The show highlighted Talma and Servais's combined talents, joy, and commitment to pushing magic in new directions with flair, originality, and excitement. It celebrated Talma's talent for sleight of hand and her signature coin tricks. All her training and experience as a solo artist culminated in this show that displayed her versatility, comedy, and conjuring skills.

PRESENTING...
LEROY, TALMA, AND BOSCO!

Servais, Talma, and Bosco stepped onto the stage to loud applause! With a flourish, the show began with Servais pulling two rabbits out of a hat. Talma strolled onto the stage, taking the hat from Servais and pulling a duck out from the same hat! Servais took back the hat from her, waved his hand over it, and this time made three rabbits appear! Cheers from the crowd! For another illusion, Servais placed Talma inside a wooden cabinet. He covered the front of the cabinet with a sheet. Then he pulled the sheet away to reveal that Talma had disappeared! To the crowd's surprise, Talma suddenly reappeared at the front of the stage, daintily fanning herself. The audience watched in awe. The third member of the trio, Bosco, the comic magician, appeared onstage next to Talma. She casually handed him the fan. He clumsily took it from her, and it immediately broke apart. Embarrassed, he awkwardly handed it back to her. She smiled and then *magically* made the fan whole again and went back to

daintily fanning herself. The nonstop magic continued with Servais returning to the stage. This time, he reached into his hat and pulled out a handful of handkerchiefs. As he counted them, they multiplied into more than seventy handkerchiefs. Bosco reappeared at that moment in an attempt to clean up the messy pile of handkerchiefs. While trying to clear the stage, he turned what had been seventy handkerchiefs into more than 200! The entertainment continued at breakneck speed when Talma now appeared in front of the curtain to perform Miser's Dream, the coin trick that she had perfected as a solo artist in which she pulled silver and gold coins from thin air to the delight of the audience.

The show raced forward when Servais then brought out a large tambourine. In an instant, he pulled silk ribbons and flags from it. But there was more. Doves, ducks, rabbits, chickens, roosters, geese, and even a large turkey emerged from the tambourine until the stage was transformed into a veritable farmyard! A grander illusion followed when Talma was dropped into a large cage with a full-grown lion! In a puff of smoke, the lion vanished!

Finally, the most popular illusion of all. A duck was placed inside the folds of a newspaper that Servais was holding. It instantly vanished. Inexplicably, more ducks appeared onstage. Servais dramatically waved a flag over them, and they too vanished. But still more feathered friends emerged from a round tub that had been placed centerstage. They flapped their wings, splashing water everywhere, and scrambled onto the floor. It didn't stop there. Thirty more ducks crawled their way out of the same tub! For the finale, a row of quacking ducks waddled offstage, one at a time. A few even returned to take a bow!

The audience cheered as the three masterful conjurers appeared onstage to a standing ovation!

THE LADY VANISHES
(1902)

Of all the illusions that Talma performed with Servais and the World's Monarchs of Magic, the most awe-inspiring was the Asrah Levitation. It set the bar for what magic would look like in the future. Servais's inventive mind working in concert with his beautiful and talented muse, Talma, created an effect that sent shock waves throughout the world.

The idea for the Asrah Levitation came about after a chance remark by Bosco, the comedian in the trio. One night, Servais and Bosco were working on a sleight of hand trick where a playing card floated through the air. Bosco joked that if Servais could make a card float in the air, why not a woman? That clicked with Servais. He knew immediately the idea could work but didn't know just how yet. He began to explore the core principles of levitating a card but on a larger scale.

At first, he doubted if an audience would ever believe such an effect. Within a few weeks, he had created a method to test the illusion with a woman assistant. He named it the Mystery of Lhassa. A perfectionist, he wasn't happy with the results and shelved the idea for five years. He brought it out again in 1902 to perform at an engagement at the Empire Theater in Johannesburg, South Africa. Talma, now thirty-four years old, had practiced the daring illusion for months leading up to the show. The night finally arrived. Bosco stood in the wings of the theater with a tray of crockery, including plates, glasses, and bowls. If the illusion failed, the plan was to distract the audience by running onstage, tripping and falling and sending the plates, cups, and bowls onto the floor while Servais handled the mishap. There was no need for the misdirection. It went off perfectly. Six weeks later, Talma performed the levitation at the famed Alhambra Theatre in her hometown of London. Bosco stood in the wings with a tray of crockery in hand. Once again, there was no need for assistance from backstage. Servais and Talma performed the illusion, the **Asrah Levitation**, without a hitch. Talma was flawless! She was the first magician to levitate and vanish in midair. It was described as the greatest illusion ever seen!

PRESENTING
THE ASRAH LEVITATION
THE SETUP

1. Servais stepped onto the stage and introduced the illusion.
2. Talma appeared, dressed in a long, flowing gown.
3. Servais hypnotized her until she fell into a deep trance.
4. Talma was then lifted onto a table and covered with a white silk sheet.
5. Music began as Talma slowly floated into the air, rising eight feet above the stage floor!

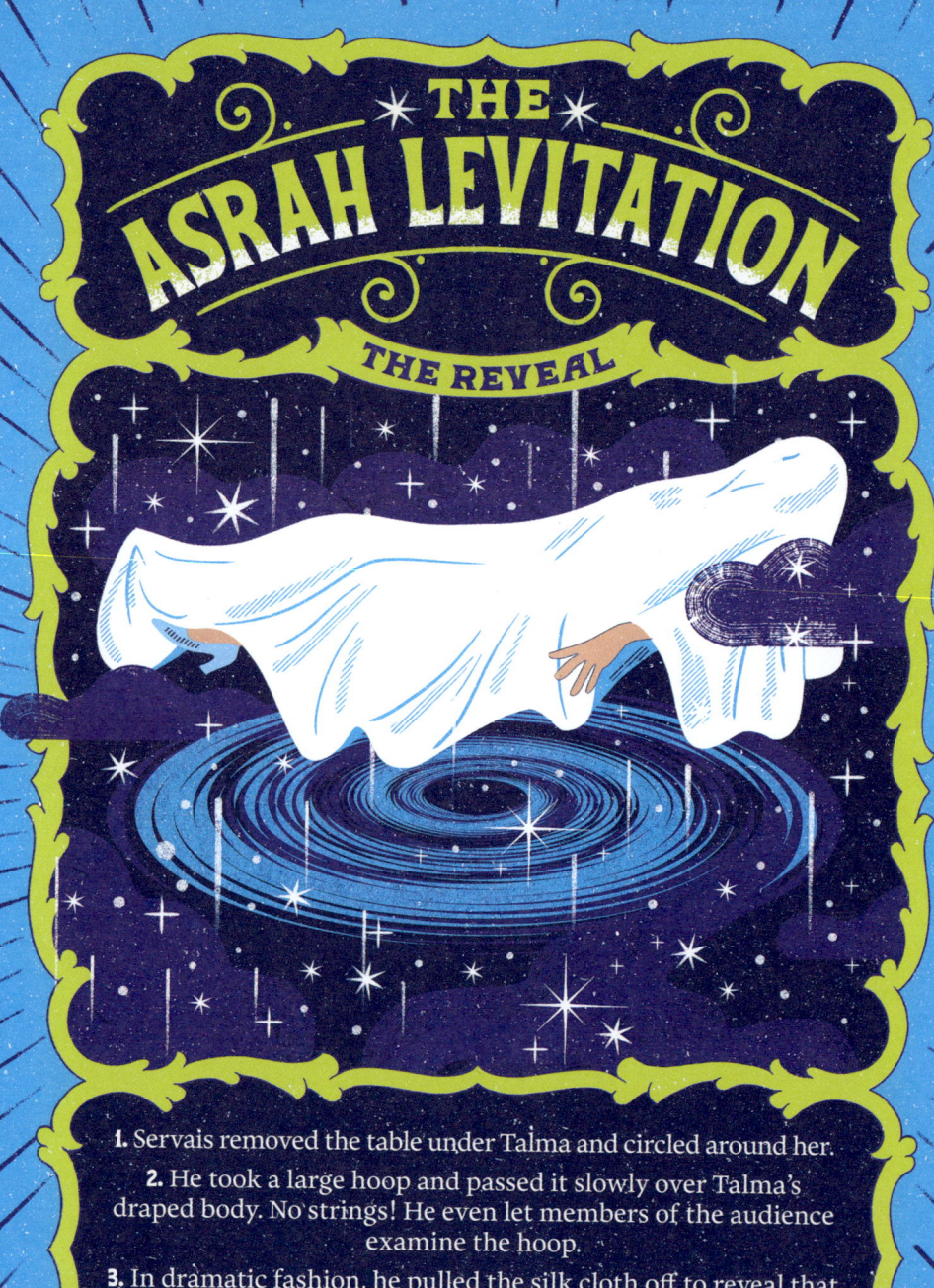

THE ASRAH LEVITATION

THE REVEAL

1. Servais removed the table under Talma and circled around her.

2. He took a large hoop and passed it slowly over Talma's draped body. No strings! He even let members of the audience examine the hoop.

3. In dramatic fashion, he pulled the silk cloth off to reveal that Talma had now disappeared!

4. From the wings, Talma entered the stage to the astonishment of the crowd.

Since the illusion was so novel and spectacular, Talma and Servais feared the trick would be imitated. They kept it a secret for a few years after the first levitation until a key component of the trick was stolen from a locked box at a theater in Paris. The identity of the thief has remained a mystery.

THE ACCIDENT
(1930)

Throughout the early 1900s, the World's Monarchs of Magic toured the world with two baggage cars of illusions, a troupe of assistants, a menagerie of livestock, and a lion! They traveled throughout Europe, Africa, and Australia, performing to sold-out audiences in popular venues. They entertained state officials, celebrities, kings, and queens. By 1930, Talma and Servais had truly become the royalty of magic. Talma established her place in magic history not only as a solo woman artist but as an equal partner with equal billing to two male magicians in their unprecedented trio act.

By this time, Talma and Servais had settled into a home in Keansburg, New Jersey, which they used as their suburban retreat between bookings. They stored their illusions, props, scenery, and costumes at their home and in a nearby warehouse. While in Keansburg, Talma and Servais enjoyed the company of other magicians who frequently visited. They treasured the quiet life away from the hectic pace of touring.

All that changed, when, on October 19, 1930, Servais was struck by a car while crossing the street in New York City. He sustained serious injuries, including a fractured skull and several broken ribs. After a long recovery, Servais recognized that he would never be the same. He had lost his dexterity and speed and the quick wit that had defined his performances. His life as a magician was over. On the same day Servais retired from the stage, Talma stopped performing magic and never looked back. She made the life-changing decision to give up one love for another.

LEGACY

(1930—1944)

Talma died peacefully in Keansburg on July 13, 1944. She had dedicated herself to the art of magic and to her husband, the genius magician Servais LeRoy. Together, they ignited the stage and inspired each other. They lived to entertain and share their gifts, inventions, and talents with the world.

Talma chose a free-spirited life on the road as a performer, contrary to the expectations of the time when women played a subservient role in marriage and in society. Talma was never just a pretty face either. In the realm of coin manipulation magic, Talma had few equals. Houdini called her the greatest sleight of hand performer who ever lived. She showed the world that women magicians could do more than float in the air. They could soar, change the rules, and challenge how magic was performed and who performed it. One of her signature coin tricks, Talma's Traveling Coin, remains a

staple in modern magicians' repertoires. Her story paved the way for women magicians who dared to break out of the box jumper role and step into the spotlight. Talma lived a life of pure magic!

LE ROY ★ TALMA ★ BOSCO

LE ROYS
INCREDIBLY MARVELLOUS
EFFECT.

THE GREATEST
LEVITATION MYSTERY
EVER SHOWN.

SERVAIS LE ROY

THE TRIPLE ALLIANCE OF MAGICIANS COMING TO THE MAJESTIC

LEROY, TALMA AND BOSCO.

RVAIS LE ROY Co
Hatton Garden
LONDON

New Illusions
ORIGINAL
SECRETS

WE
ORIGINATE
NOT
IMITATE

LARGEST
MAGIC
SHOPS
IN THE WORL

MA ★ BOSCO

TALMA
LEROY-TALMA-BOSCO

BEATRICE HOUDINI

THE MESSENGER

JANUARY 23, 1876 – FEBRUARY 11, 1943

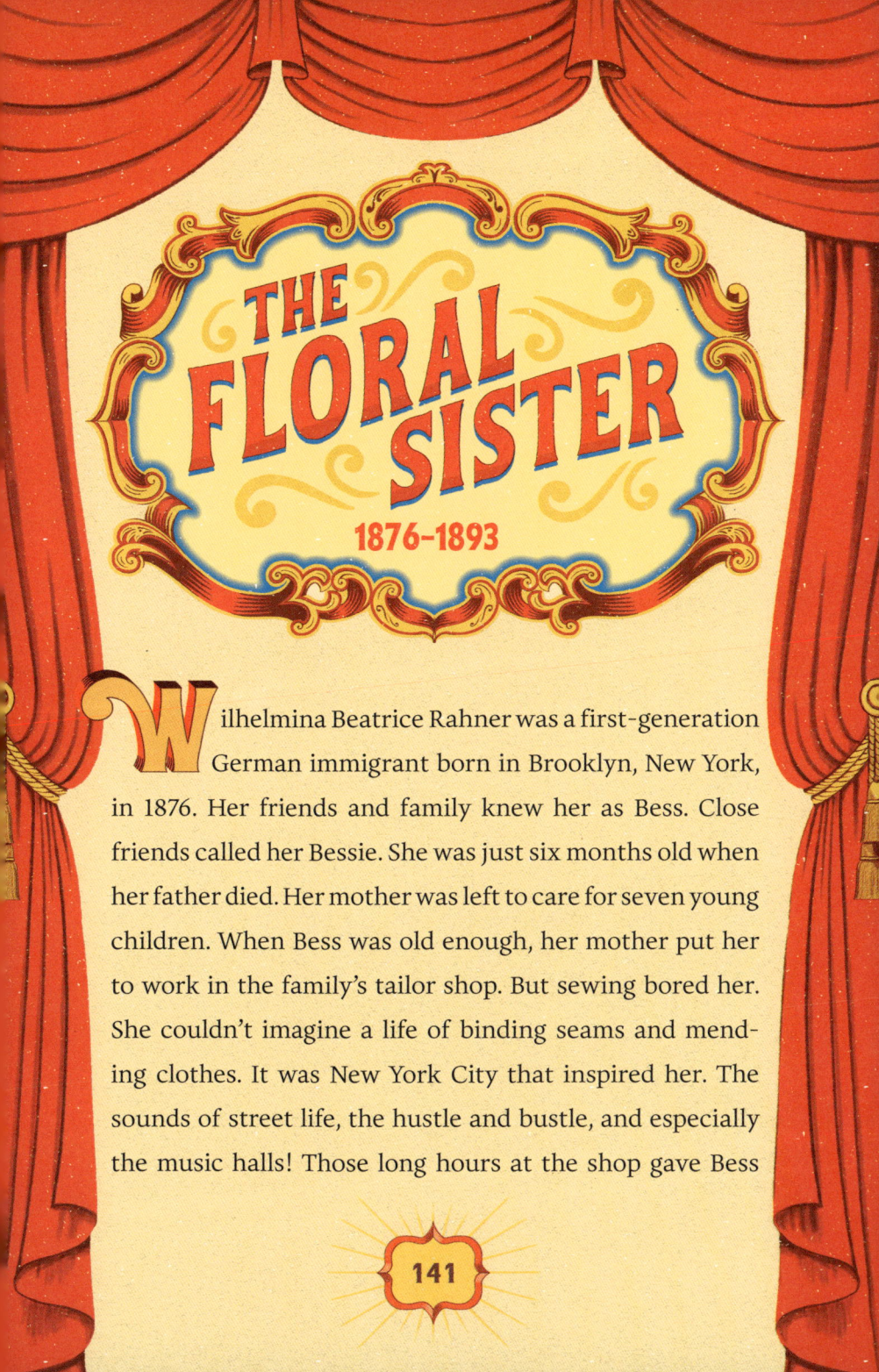

THE FLORAL SISTER

1876–1893

Wilhelmina Beatrice Rahner was a first-generation German immigrant born in Brooklyn, New York, in 1876. Her friends and family knew her as Bess. Close friends called her Bessie. She was just six months old when her father died. Her mother was left to care for seven young children. When Bess was old enough, her mother put her to work in the family's tailor shop. But sewing bored her. She couldn't imagine a life of binding seams and mending clothes. It was New York City that inspired her. The sounds of street life, the hustle and bustle, and especially the music halls! Those long hours at the shop gave Bess time to dream. Soon she knew exactly what she wanted to do. Sing and dance under the bright lights! Whenever she could, she escaped to watch shows in nearby Coney Island, a lively seaside boardwalk in Brooklyn lined with variety acts.

By her late teens, Bess had grown tired of living in her family's crowded apartment under the strict rules of her mother. One day, she ditched work, changed her name to Bessie Raymond, and ran away from home. Like Anna Eva Fay, Adelaide Herrmann, Dixie Haygood, and Mary Ann Ford, Bess made the bold decision to risk it all to follow her dream. She was determined to start a new life in show business! Within days, Bess landed her first opportunity, washing dishes and mending costumes for one of the traveling acts she had admired from the front row. There, she met two other teenage girl performers from the troupe who shared her ambitions for the spotlight. They formed a song-and-dance act, calling themselves the Floral Sisters. Before long, they were performing at small venues around Coney Island. Bess had begun her stage career during a time when the streets were alive with a mix of cultures from waves of immigrants coming from Europe to America with the hope of a better life. Bess's own dreams were born in this vibrant Brooklyn community against the electric backdrop of urban development, economic expansion, and the rise of vaudeville. And now, at eighteen years old, Bessie Raymond was about to introduce herself to the world as a professional singer and dancer. Her dream was coming true!

A CONEY ISLAND COURTSHIP
(1894)

While performing at the Sea Beach Palace in Coney Island, Bess met a young magician named Theo Weiss. They began dating. One evening, Theo brought along his older brother, Ehrich, to join them for dinner. Theo and Ehrich were performing a popular magic act at the time called the Brothers Houdini. Ehrich's stage name was Harry Houdini! The act had been gaining attention in the dime museums on the Coney Island boardwalk. In the late nineteenth century, a dime museum was a theatrical showcase of oddities and variety acts featuring sword swallowers, fire eaters, strongmen, jugglers, and magicians performing for a ten-cent admission. These museums were aimed at the working class, in direct contrast to the upscale fine art museums in neighboring Manhattan.

On that June evening in 1894, the moment Bess set eyes on Harry, it was love at first sight. Theo recognized their mutual infatuation and graciously stepped aside. Harry was nineteen, a year older than Bess. The two became inseparable. One afternoon, after a full day of amusement on Coney Island's boardwalk, Harry and Bess passed by a secondhand jewelry store. Harry whisked Bess inside. He asked her to marry him on the spot! After she accepted, he told her to pick out any ring in the store and it would be hers. When she picked out a ring, Harry sheepishly revealed that he had no money left in his pocket. Bess ended up paying for the engagement ring herself!

Two weeks later, Bess and Harry Houdini were married. Bess insisted that, since she was Catholic and Harry was Jewish, they needed to hold two ceremonies—one with a priest presiding and one with a rabbi officiating. Despite the Catholic wedding, Bess's mother did not accept Harry into the family. She disapproved of Bess marrying so hastily, and to a showman at that! Since Bess and Harry were still so young when they married, Harry's mother, Cecilia, embraced the couple and took them into the Weisses' crowded tenement apartment until they were able to make a proper living on their own.

Harry had been practicing and performing magic since he was a child. At sixteen, he had changed his name to Harry Houdini and dedicated his life to magic after reading the memoirs of innovative French magician Jean-Eugène Robert-Houdin. Harry's drive and ambition matched Bess's desire to escape poverty and pursue a career in show business. Bess and Harry shared the same romantic view of a life on the road as performers. Their marriage was founded on love and admiration but quickly broadened into a dynamic creative and business partnership. Soon after they took their vows, Harry and Theo broke up their brother act. Before handing the wand over to Bess, Harry insisted that she and Theo make a pledge that they remain loyal to him throughout their lives. After the dramatic midnight declaration under a cloudy Coney Island sky, Harry began to share his magic secrets with Bess. Soon she became Harry's key accomplice in the art of deception.

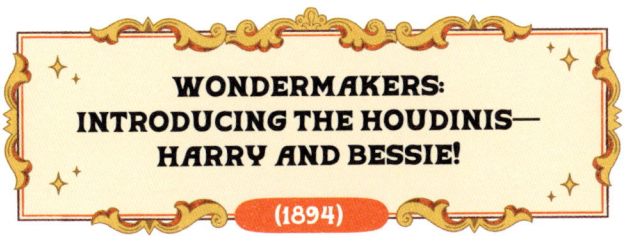

WONDERMAKERS: INTRODUCING THE HOUDINIS— HARRY AND BESSIE!

(1894)

Bess grew up superstitious and wary of magic as a child. Her stern mother convinced all her children of the evils of entertainers and wondermakers. She insisted they stay away from the devil's playground—show business! Even though Bess had stage experience as a singer and dancer, performing magic was new to her. In Bess and Harry's mad rush to get married, Harry realized that he had never asked Bess her father's name. One evening, he told her to write down the name of her father on a piece of paper. He then instructed her to crumple it up and hand it to him. He took the paper, burned it, and rubbed the ashes on his forearm. Suddenly, her father's name appeared written on his arm in what seemed to be red blood. Bess couldn't believe her eyes. She worried that maybe her mother was right. Was Harry Houdini the devil? Harry calmed her down and proceeded to explain how the trick was done before she let her superstitions send her running out of the apartment.

Just as Anna Eva Fay's honeymoon was more of an apprenticeship under Henry Melville than a romantic getaway, Harry took Bess under his wing and started magic lessons right away. A seasoned magician carefully chooses who to share secrets with, and it's traditionally a trusted family member or a loyal apprentice. Magic legacy is at stake with every trick that is shared. A woman rarely had access to these mysteries unless she was married to a magician or the daughter of one. Harry trusted Bess and believed in their love and future together. He began to teach her his repertoire of card tricks, sleight of hand, mind reading, and fortunetelling. When she was ready, she tested the waters by assisting Harry on small stages at Coney Island's dime museums, with rowdy and boisterous crowds often interrupting their act. The Houdinis gained a following and began to secure more bookings and perform as many as ten shows a day, starting at ten a.m. and ending at ten p.m. During this period, they had no home of their own. They lived out of their suitcase and prop trunk. With each engagement, they were given small furnished rooms. Wherever they toured, Harry woke up at five in the morning and made coffee for them before they started their day. In those early hours, he sometimes took walks and imagined ways to expand their act. That was his dreaming time.

For the shows on their first tour, Bess opened with a song-and-dance routine. Harry followed with a handcuff escape, a trick he had perfected as a child. He then performed card tricks and other sleight of hand illusions, including an audience favorite called the Needles Trick, in which he swallowed twenty to thirty stainless steel needles along with a single piece of thread. Once a volunteer from the audience confirmed that there was nothing in his mouth, Harry then slowly pulled the needles out to reveal that they were now all tied together on the same long thread.

Harry understood the power of publicity from the beginning. He made sure to promote the duo's image as professional entertainers with early press photos depicting him wearing a formal overcoat and top hat and carrying a cane, while Bess smiled demurely at the camera dressed in black tights and bloomers with simple strapped low-heeled shoes. On tour, Bess discovered Harry's knack for capturing a headline when one day she came across a newspaper ad. The ad bet anyone $100 that Harry could escape any set of handcuffs put before him. It was signed "Harry Houdini, Handcuff King and Jail-Breaker." Bess was horrified! What if he failed? How could they afford to make good on the challenge? Harry quickly explained that he had been setting aside money from their performances. Bess wrote to her sister Stella about the stunt. Stella couldn't believe that her little sister had become so wealthy. When Bess's mother heard the news, she fainted. She was now convinced that Bess had not only married the devil but a jail-breaker too!

TRANSFORMATION

(1894)

The Houdinis' charismatic personalities combined with their exceptional magic skills attracted bigger crowds to each show. New bookings led them to the South and Midwest. They soon landed engagements all along the East Coast in celebrated venues such as Keith's in Boston and Tony Pastor's in New York. For their popular act, Bess also put her seamstress skills to work designing and sewing all the costumes. The trick that brought the most attention was called **Metamorphosis**. Bess stood four feet, nine inches tall and weighed under 100 pounds. Her petite frame suited the illusion perfectly!

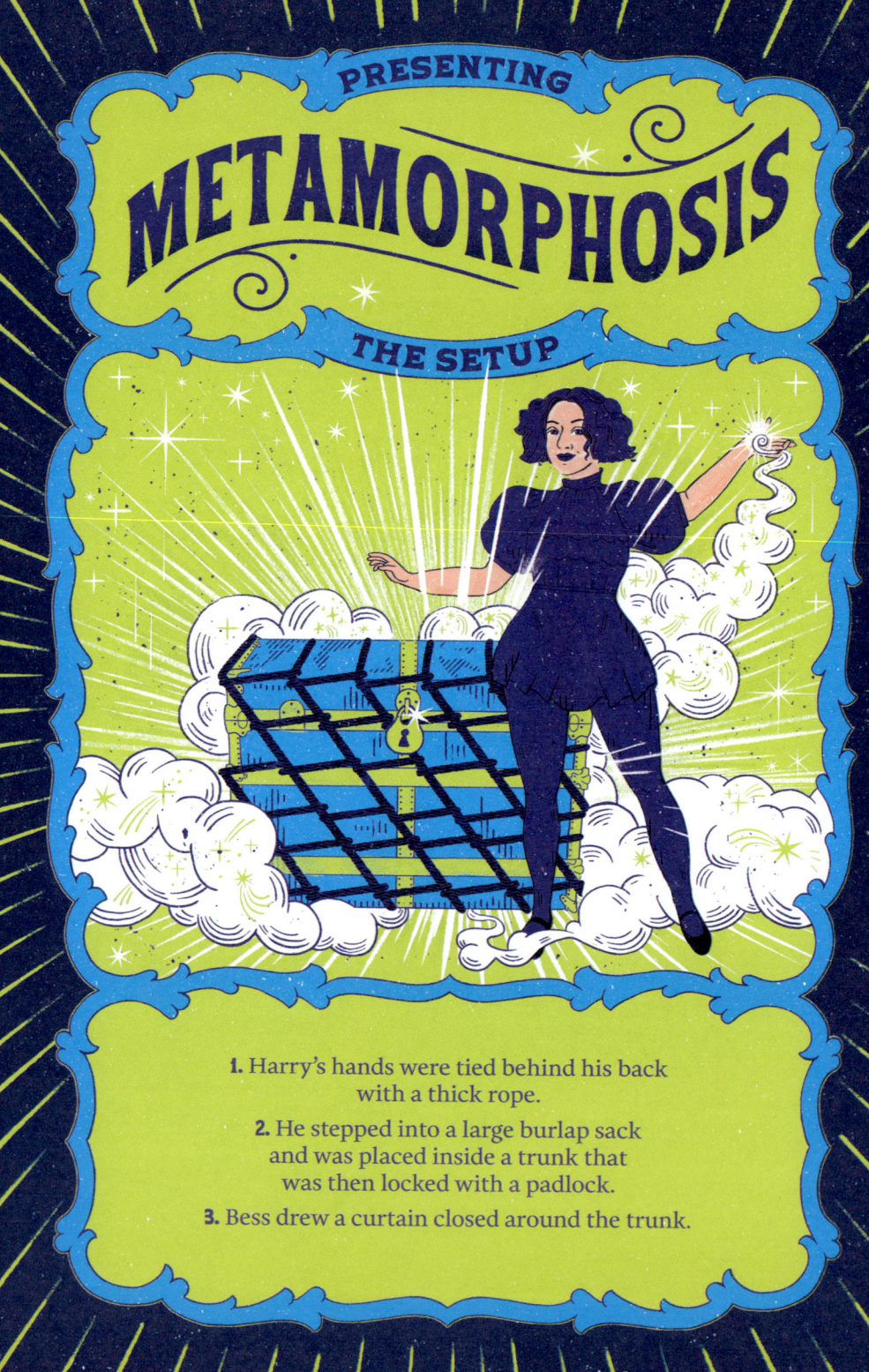

PRESENTING

METAMORPHOSIS

THE SETUP

1. Harry's hands were tied behind his back with a thick rope.

2. He stepped into a large burlap sack and was placed inside a trunk that was then locked with a padlock.

3. Bess drew a curtain closed around the trunk.

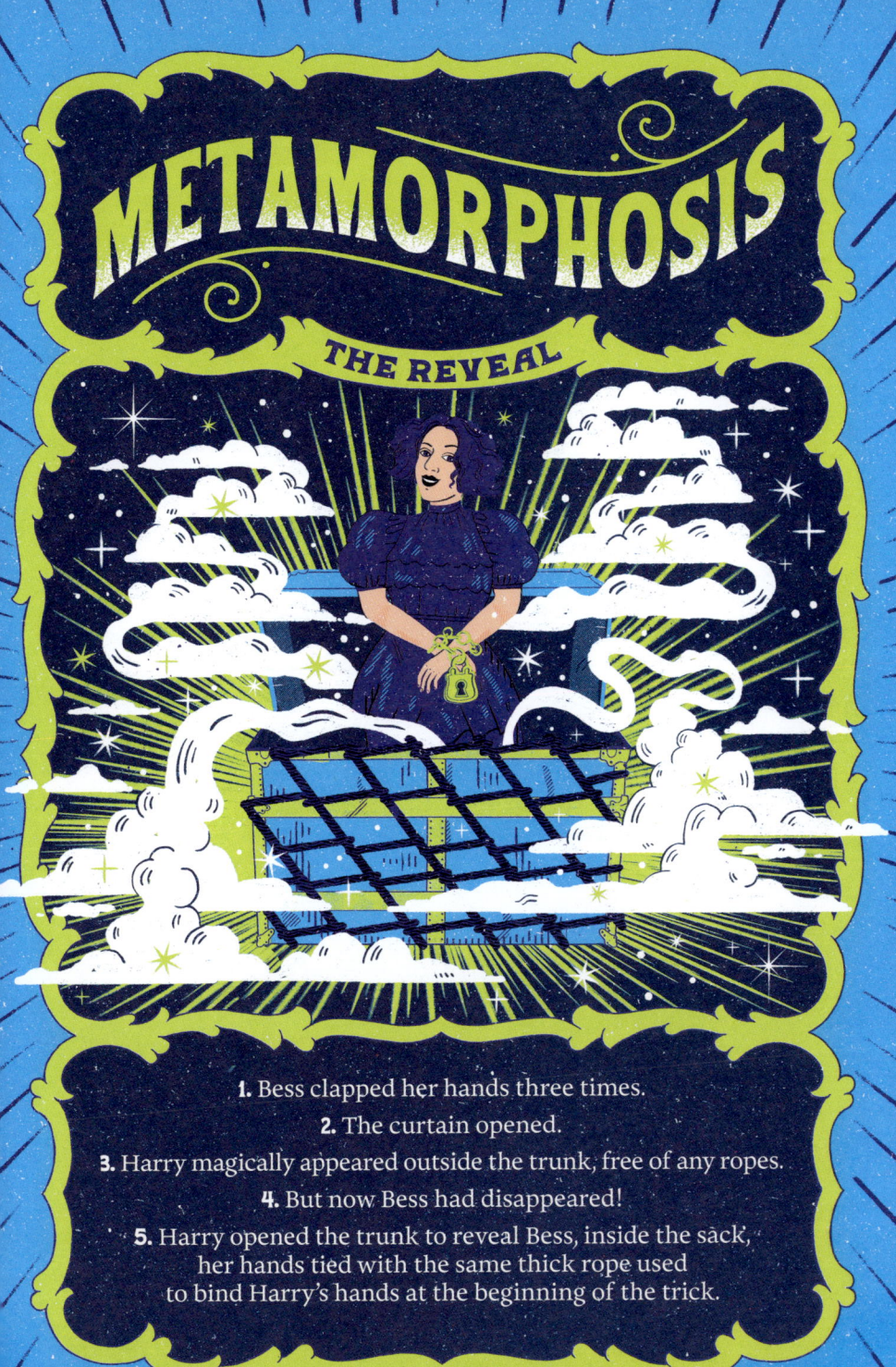

METAMORPHOSIS

THE REVEAL

1. Bess clapped her hands three times.

2. The curtain opened.

3. Harry magically appeared outside the trunk, free of any ropes.

4. But now Bess had disappeared!

5. Harry opened the trunk to reveal Bess, inside the sack, her hands tied with the same thick rope used to bind Harry's hands at the beginning of the trick.

The Houdinis claimed the switch took only three seconds! It was an awe-inspiring illusion. Yet, even with positive press about Metamorphosis, the young couple struggled to make ends meet. They needed to keep developing their act to attract more attention, making it bigger and more outlandish.

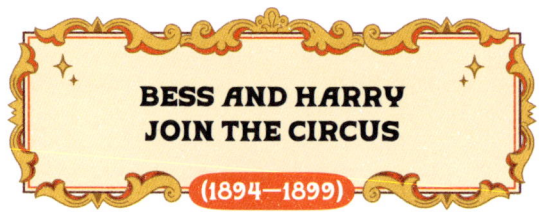

BESS AND HARRY JOIN THE CIRCUS

(1894—1899)

Bess and Harry's first break came when they were asked to join the Welsh Brothers Circus troupe. The opportunity brought steady work and a regular paycheck. Three meals a day and $25 a week! For extra cash, Bess sang in the act and Harry sold bars of soap to troupe members. Traveling with the circus meant living in tight quarters and often under harsh conditions. This caused tension between the couple. Their strong and fiery personalities clashed despite their devotion to each other. Whenever they had an argument, they arranged that Harry would leave and take a walk. When he returned, he opened the door and tossed his hat into the room. If Bess didn't throw back the hat, all was forgiven. But if Bess threw the hat back out the door, Harry had to take another walk around the block until tensions cooled!

By the end of the busy circus season, Bess and Harry had saved enough money to take time off from touring and return to their families in New York. Their time off-stage didn't last long. To survive as magicians required constant promotion and reinvention to stay ahead of the competition. The Houdinis needed to push themselves in new directions. They decided to add a Spiritualist act next and called it Professor and Mademoiselle Houdini, the Occult Expositors. The new act caught the attention of a promoter, Dr. Thomas Hill, who offered Bess and Harry a spot in a traveling medicine show with other vaudevillians. The troupe included the Keaton family, whose young son Buster became a household name in early Hollywood films. Bess and Harry joined Dr. Hill's California Concert Company. They peddled bottled miracle cures during daylight hours and performed their stage act in the evening.

It was now 1898, and while on tour with the medicine show, business began to slow. Dr. Hill asked the Houdinis to stage a public séance to help drum up more business. The troupe was set to perform at the local Opera House in Galena, Kansas. The advertisement read, "Houdini the Great Will Give a Spirit Séance on Sunday in the Open Light." It promised a night of mystery. To prepare, Harry visited the town's graveyard and gathered local gossip from the groundskeeper. From his morning research, he uncovered the names, dates, and stories about the town's history. Bess had learned the deceptive art of minding reading from Harry. She was ready to assist him. Before the séance, Harry reviewed the secret code system he had shared with Bess, which included signals and spoken words presented in a variety of ways. During the act, Harry might change the position of his hands and feet, or even alter his facial expression to communicate cues to Bess in a crowded theater. The "séance" was a triumph! In fact, the performance was perhaps a little too convincing. Two local businessmen approached Harry backstage to offer him $25 if he and Bess promised to never conduct a séance in their town again!

When the medicine show tour ended, the Houdinis returned to performing with the Welsh Circus for another six-month tour. During these early years, Bess learned how to navigate the unpredictability of life as a working magician. In Harry's mind, the future was brighter than ever despite the fact that the couple still depended on their next booking to survive. Bess shared Harry's drive and enthusiasm, even in the face of their financial struggles. It had been her dream to embark on an adventurous life in show business. She and Harry supported each other and knew in their hearts that success was inevitable. It was just a matter of time.

ESCAPING TO FAME AND FORTUNE

By the early 1900s, Harry's fascination with escape had deepened. In every town where Bess and Harry toured their act, Harry scouted police stations. He publicly challenged the local authorities, claiming that he could break out of any set of handcuffs or any jail cell anywhere, anytime. With each dare, he stirred up interest and built intrigue. During this early period in Harry's escapes, he and Bess worked as a team. Before each stunt, Bess distracted the policemen at the station while Harry snuck in to assess the handcuffs and jail cells so he could devise an escape strategy. As in any trick or illusion, preparation was key to a successful outcome, even if it meant breaking the law!

The public escapes Harry performed town to town separated him from other magicians at the time. Because of the growing interest in Harry as a solo artist, Bess and Harry agreed that they would focus on Harry's theatrical escapes as the centerpiece of their show. Bess would shift to a more behind-the-scenes role. In hopes of gaining a larger audience, they decided to take the money they had earned from their recent tours and travel across the Atlantic to Europe. At the turn of the twentieth century, if an act succeeded in London, Paris, or Berlin, the common belief in magic circles was that an even bigger American audiences would follow.

Bess and Harry traveled across the ocean without a single booking lined up in Europe. After a rough ocean journey that left Bess nursing Harry's seasickness for most of the trip, the couple finally arrived in London. They immediately got to work trying desperately to track down booking agents. After weeks of one rejection after another, Harry met a young manager who challenged him to a dare. If Harry could escape Scotland Yard handcuffs, the manager would hire him for two weeks at the famed Alhambra Theatre. Scotland Yard was—and still is—the headquarters of the highly respected police force of greater London. Harry relished the challenge! And, to the astonishment of the Scotland Yard police and the booking agent, Harry successfully broke free! Soon after the handcuff escape, the Houdinis began a two-week engagement. The show was an instant success and led to an extended stay through the following summer. With cash in his pocket,

Houdini bought his beloved mother, Cecilia, a dress that had been custom-made for Queen Victoria, who had just passed away. The dress symbolized the Houdinis' journey from the dime museum shows on Coney Island. Harry's royal gift was a gesture to his mother and a grand thank-you for believing in him and Bess and their commitment to a life of magic.

Word of mouth spread. Soon the duo received invitations to perform throughout Europe and even as far as Russia. While on tour, Harry expanded the act. A student of magic, he endlessly researched ways of improving his techniques, experimenting and challenging himself with new daring escapes. He learned to open locked safes, escape packing boxes, and free himself from straitjackets. With each successful escape, Harry grew increasingly popular. Thousands of spectators began to show up only to be turned away. In all his demonstrations, there wasn't a single failure. After four years of capturing headlines and winning over audiences across Europe, Harry and Bess returned home to America as celebrities, just as they had hoped.

Although it was invisible to the public, Bess had orchestrated Harry's rise to fame. She handled all the financial and practical aspects of the show, including the props, costumes, and sets that Harry had added to the act. She performed a key role by managing the bookings and business side of the partnership. She and Harry soon began to enjoy the fruits of their success. They stayed at luxury hotels, ate well, and when they returned to New York, Bess even took her first cab ride! Bess's biggest challenge now wasn't how she could afford her next meal but how she could contain Harry's extravagant spending—particularly on magic memorabilia and artifacts. By the time Bess and Harry purchased their first home in uptown New York City, Harry had amassed such a large magic collection that he created a dedicated library just for his books, playbills, newspapers, programs, and photographs. Despite Bess's warnings, there was no limit to Harry's expenditures. He rarely knew how much money he had at any given time and never carried cash in his pockets.

Over time, Houdini's escapes became more dangerous and spectacular. Bess found it difficult to watch him risk his life in front of screaming crowds. On many occasions, she withdrew to the quiet of her home or hotel room to plan the details of the next tour, sew costumes, do needlepoint, and read romance novels. She began to long for a simpler life and took up doll collecting, which helped calm her nerves while Harry entertained crowds by hanging off the sides of buildings or diving off bridges into freezing cold rivers.

In 1913, Harry's beloved mother, Cecilia, died unexpectedly of a stroke. Harry loved her dearly and found it difficult to live without her. He became obsessed with visiting mediums in an attempt to contact Cecilia in the great beyond. During his desperate search for a sign from his mother, he visited over 100 mediums. None could deliver a message. Devastated, his pain turned to anger, and he staged relentless attacks against Spiritualists and mediums. He spent the rest of his life lecturing and exposing fraudulent mediums wherever he could.

THE HOUDINI CODE

Throughout Harry's campaign to fight mediums, part of him still held out hope that there might be an afterlife. He and Bess made a pledge that whoever passed away first would send a message back to the other to prove or disprove that spirit communication existed. The message was known as the Houdini Code. The secret phrase was "Rosabelle, believe," from a lyric of the first song Houdini heard Bess sing as a Floral Sister.

160

A LOVE STORY

After Harry's mother's death, he poured all his devotion into Bess. He wrote her a love letter every day. Each morning, while Bess still slept, he composed sweet, romantic messages and left them on her pillow or on her dresser or somewhere in their apartment or hotel room. The notes usually began and ended with an affectionate phrase.

One of his notes read:

Adorable Sunshine of my Life
I have had my coffee, have washed out the
glass, and am on my way to business.
—Houdini
My darling, I love you

Bess and Harry loved each other unconditionally and rarely separated. When Bess discovered that she couldn't have children, it was a source of deep sorrow for the couple. Yet she and Harry found a way to build an extended family around them, with nieces and nephews to fill the void. As Harry's fame grew, Bess supported his spectacular career. Harry's fame fed her celebrity lifestyle too. When the bill called for it, Bess returned to the stage with Harry, reviving her roles in Metamorphosis and in their mind-reading act.

Bess always believed in Harry's vision and shared his passion for magic. Magic had brought them together and taken them around the world meeting dukes, kings, queens, presidents, and popular personalities of the time. Bess had seen and experienced a world bigger than she could have ever dreamed of as a young girl.

HALLOWEEN

(1926)

In 1926, there were many new plans in the works. Harry had enrolled at Columbia University to get a college degree. He had developed a new act and was working on his latest stunt, a trick where he was planning to escape from inside a giant block of ice in front of a live audience!

While Harry and Bess were on their latest tour, Harry fractured his ankle. He insisted on going on with the performance. He even devised his own brace to help secure the ankle. At the next stop, Harry visited McGill University in Montreal, Canada, to lecture on Spiritualism. After the lecture, an art student showed him a portrait he had drawn of him. Impressed, Harry invited him to come backstage a few days later at the Princess Theater, where he would be performing. The student brought along a few friends that night. While Harry rested his ankle, lounging on the dressing room couch, he casually talked with the students. One of the student's was named J. Gordon Whitehead. Whitehead asked Harry questions about his extraordinary strength and physical endurance. Harry explained that whenever his strength was tested, he had to first brace and position himself for the blow. Without warning, Whitehead punched Harry four times in the stomach. After the fourth blow, Harry stopped him, and the young men left. Even though Harry felt discomfort, he went on with the performance that night. He continued with two more shows over the next two days until he could no longer withstand the pain. When the doctors finally diagnosed the injury, they discovered that Harry had suffered a ruptured appendix that had developed into a life-threatening infection. On October 31, 1926, Harry passed away in Bess's arms.

After Harry died, Bess found a final note from him.

> Sweetheart, when you read this I shall be dead. Dear Heart, do not grieve; I shall be at rest by the side of my beloved parents, and wait for you always—remember! I loved only two women in my life: my mother and my wife. Yours, in Life, Death, and Ever After.

Harry had left the bulk of the monetary and material effects to Bess. Bess also became the beneficiary of insurance policies that had been paid out to her because of Houdini's accidental death. She now found herself at a crossroads, not knowing what her life would look like without the great Harry Houdini by her side. How could she survive without him? Alone now, she needed to rebuild a life for herself. After a time of mourning, she returned to singing and dancing onstage in a vaudeville act. She staged the ice stunt that Harry had imagined on Broadway, which was short-lived. She opened a teahouse in New York City and continued to travel and make appearances in Harry's honor. Somehow, she found a way to live her life on her own terms without Harry. Throughout it all, she never lost track of her deep responsibility to the magic world as the wife of a legend.

THE FINAL SÉANCE

(1936)

Every Sunday at noon, Bess locked herself in a dark room lit only by a single candle. She sat beneath a framed portrait of Harry waiting for the coded message that she and Harry had agreed upon together. No message ever came. After privately mourning Harry for ten years, Bess decided to stage a public séance on live radio with spirit circles formed around the world. Dignitaries and celebrities joined her at the Knickerbocker Hotel in the heart of Hollywood on Halloween night in 1936, exactly ten years after Harry's untimely death. Now the world would wait for a sign from the great beyond. Harry's spirit never materialized. Bess blew out the single candle that night and whispered, "Good night, Harry."

You are invited to attend

Final **Houdini** Seance

8:30 to 9:00 P. M.

October Thirty-first, Nineteen hundred thirty-six

(Hallowe'en)

EDWARD SAINT
DIRECTOR FINAL SEANCE

THE QUIET MESSENGER

(1936—1943)

Bess continued to find ways to keep Harry's memory and influence over the magic community alive. She attended and appeared at many ceremonies and engagements commemorating his legacy. In 1939, she turned her attention to highlighting the role of women in magic. She helped form the first woman's magic club of its kind, Magigals, with the goal of mentoring aspiring women magicians.

166

Then, in 1943, while on a cross-country train trip to New York City, she passed away peacefully at sixty-seven years old. Bess Houdini was a quiet messenger who carefully curated an essential piece of magic history for future generations of magicians and magic enthusiasts. Her own legacy as a performer and influential creative force behind the most famous magician in the world is often overlooked and undervalued. Since her passing, Bess's pivotal role in magic history has all but disappeared.

THE MESSENGER

TONIGHT
Wednesday, April 7th
At B. F. KEITH'S

HOUDINI

The Wizard of the World has

ON THE BOARD WALK (BRIGHTON) CONEY ISLAND, N.Y.

O. L. Bauer.   Joe Deisel.
Harry Crum

GET SEATS EARLY

London,
Wis

an
Mr. & Mrs.

Month of January, 1903, at
Rembrandt Theatre, Amsterdam, Holland.

Mr & Mrs Houdini
— Wishing you many
happy returns of the
Day.
Mr. Harry Kellar

"...GES"
...NI FAIL
...HIS CODE

(AP) — Harry ... lied on Octo- ... ets by which ... et messages ... ld, his wife

... ng 35 years ... ose fraudu- ... iums, com- ... words, of ... the knowl- ... e. Of the ... ges" which ... iums had ... r departed ... udini said ... ords that ... i's. The ... eased for

PATRONS CONCERNING ITS ... message received by a ... medium in Attleboro, Mass., on No-vember 2, which she submitted as the attempt of Houdini to get in touch with this world. The medium, who asked that her name be kept secret, used automatic writing as her means of "establishing contact," and obtained three messages, a brief one and two much longer compositions.

"Astral soul is vested at last, Weiss (Houdini's original name) says God is welcome creator—God is truth—God is love—God is without peer," one of the messages started, and ended, "See some of my friends and tell them Houdini lives."

Mrs. Houdini was reached by telephone at Atlantic City, where she is convalescing from the illness which has kept her in bed since her husband's death. The messages were read to her in full, and she denied that they contained anything similar to the quotation composed by her husband, and agreed upon by them as a means of communicating with her if communication were found possible.

...municate, he

To My Boys of the
Houdini Club of
Philadelphia
from their
Mother
Mrs. Harry Houdini

GODDESS OF WAR

1877–1900

Minerva, the Queen of Handcuffs, took on the world with the courage of Wonder Woman. She was born in Germany in 1877. Her birth name is not well documented. By some accounts, her original name was Margaretha Snelling, and by others, it was Margaretha Gertz. But when she discovered her passion for magic, she boldly renamed herself Minerva, inspired by the fierce warrior goddess who dressed in protective armor and carried a spear. Minerva performed daring jumps off high bridges into cold rivers and escaped straitjackets, padlocked trunks, and locked jail cells. Her brave step into the high-stakes world of death-defying magic stunts of the nineteenth century created a powerful image for women and men. She was the goddess of war. A heroine who could conquer our greatest fear—death!

As a young teen, Margaretha watched as the other schoolgirls around her dreamed of the day they would meet their husbands and start a family. Margaretha wasn't sure where she fit in since she knew that her future would tell a different story. Unfortunately, the opportunities for unmarried women were limited to teaching, nursing, or domestic work. None of these professions appealed to Margaretha. She felt confined by the rules of German society. A desire and an urge to break out of these conventions built up inside her. Dreams of escape consumed her.

FEARLESS REBEL

(1900—1903)

While most young women had found their match and were setting up homes, preparing meals for their children, and managing family affairs, Margaretha was focused on something else. Her future! In 1900, the great Harry Houdini had taken the world of magic performance to a new level. Minerva read of his extraordinary escapes throughout Europe with interest and enthusiasm. The image of this fearless magician connected to her own rebellious spirit and desire to set herself apart from her peers. It inspired her to dedicate her life to learning and performing magic and becoming an escape artist! Escape artists in the nineteenth century were magicians who performed daring illusions. They created a sense of danger by putting their bodies at great risk in front of live audiences. Margaretha began intensive training. She first studied the art of handcuff escape as an assistant, practicing hiding a skeleton key out of sight in the palm of her hand or up the sleeve of her dress. She then built muscles and strength to prepare for the physical challenges that lay ahead. As an escape artist, she also learned how to twist and contort her body to create the outward appearance of struggle and pain and overdramatize the danger of the stunt.

Margaretha possessed other powers besides her athleticism and performance skills. She was a natural beauty. Blond and full-figured, she played the part of the towering mythical goddess to perfection. After a period of study, she began to land work as a solo performer in small venues throughout Europe. For her act, she performed her stunts in a dress or in a blouse with a long, flowing skirt. Her hair was all done up with care and attention. She convinced the audience into thinking they were witnessing a dainty and conventional woman of the nineteenth century. When she escaped from locked handcuffs and padlocked chains with the strength of any man, they saw instead a fearless rebel turning the stereotype of the delicate female on its head. Margaretha enjoyed the feeling of freedom. She pushed her body to the limit with each escape, announcing herself to the world as Minerva, the Queen of Handcuffs!

AMERICAN QUEEN
(1903—1907)

The year Minerva turned twenty-five, she met German vaudevillian William Van Dorn. William was also an escape artist. He called himself the King of Handcuffs. He was one of a growing group of magicians riding the wave of Houdini-esque escape acts that were now in high demand in Europe. He needed to separate himself from the pack. He recognized something unique in Minerva's act, which had been gaining attention on smaller European stages. He saw a powerful woman unafraid to take risks, who performed with great confidence. She was beautiful and talented too. There was no other woman quite like her performing escapes. The King of Handcuffs offered the Queen of Handcuffs an opportunity to join forces. Minerva saw the benefit of the partnership; William could help secure bookings on larger, more popular stages that Minerva didn't have access to, since she was a solo female performer. She was ambitious and driven.

She also knew that she had more to learn in order to take her skills to a higher level. She accepted William's business proposal. The Queen and King of Handcuffs became the royalty of magic escapes.

William trained Minerva on the finer points of escaping handcuffs. He helped her develop the theatrical and technical skills needed to bring the illusion to its full effect. She learned how to slowly and dramatically build the suspense leading up to the escape. The idea was to capture the spectators' attention and keep them interested while creating a cloud of mystery around her extraordinary feats. Minerva thrived in her new role. She was a free spirit, developing her magic skills and performing throughout Europe. Then, unexpectedly, she found herself falling in love.

Together, Minerva and William decided to sail across the Atlantic on a steamship to try their act in America. Before beginning their tour, they took a side trip to picturesque Niagara Falls and married there. After a brief honeymoon, they began performing as an escape artist duo. They advertised themselves as both the Van Dorns and the Vanos. One reviewer called them the "transatlantic wizards of handcuffs." They performed on touring circuits in Massachusetts, Connecticut, Ohio, and New York. From the start, Minerva was the one who captured the attention of the crowd, quickly surpassing her husband's conjuring skills. Gradually, William took

Min

AM

Record Breaking

rva

ICAN QUEEN OF MYSTERY

raight Jacket Escape

on a dual role as her magic partner and her manager. Minerva's star was rising. By 1906, she had become the featured magician in the act. Jealously and competition fueled tensions between the two of them. By the 1907 touring season, Minerva had begun performing solo.

Minerva couldn't contain her fierce independent spirit. She took on bigger and more challenging illusions and expanded her act. She taught herself the straitjacket escape that rival escape artists, led by Houdini, were performing on competing stages. Being strapped in a straitjacket could be painful, and it took coordination, strength, and speed to break free without injury. If Minerva didn't free her arms quickly enough, her muscles would stiffen, and the pain would become unbearable. It took practice and discipline to perfect the skill. She didn't stop there. To keep pace with Houdini and his imitators, she taught herself how to escape jail cells, locked trunks, and padlocked chains. Minerva was on a mission to stay on top of her competition, determined to build a successful career in America on her own terms.

DARING AND DANGEROUS

(1908)

Houdini had been showcasing his death-defying stunts on a scale the public had never seen before. His sensational publicity campaigns fueled his growing fame and attracted crowds of thousands to witness his staged jail-cell breakouts and bridge jumps. His brazen showmanship drew flashy headlines. Minerva needed to catch up with Houdini's thrilling stunts to stay competitive and win over audiences. While training for more daring and dangerous illusions, she spent less time with William than she did cultivating her image as Minerva, American Queen of Mystery. She was more focused on adding spectacle to her solo act than on repairing her troubled marriage. Her escapes were the key to her personal freedom.

With Minerva's marriage on the brink of divorce, she needed to redefine her place in the magic world. She decided to attempt the Bridge Jump! One of the most daring escapes of the time. The stunt required that she train her body to stretch and bend, and control her muscles to help minimize the impact when she hit the surface of the cold water. She also learned how to swim in the unpredictable currents of the deep rivers where she would be performing. She practiced holding her breath under cold water in her bathtub just long enough to free herself from the restraints of the strait-jacket. Soon she was ready!

Presenting . . . "the American Queen of Mystery, the only woman bridge-jumper, jail-breaker, and handcuff expert in the world!" Her publicity posters promised that Minerva would be more wonderful than Houdini!

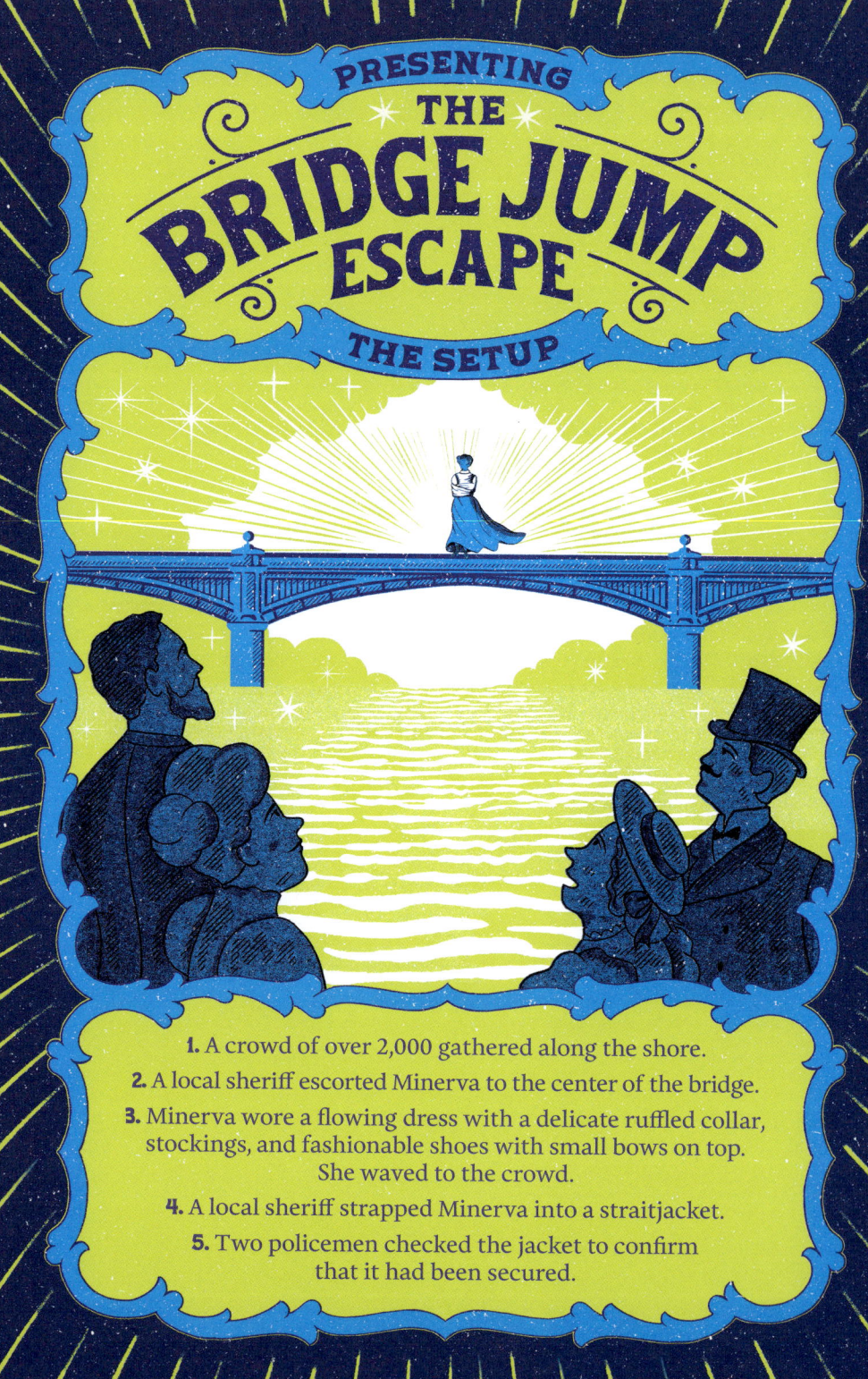

PRESENTING
THE
BRIDGE JUMP
ESCAPE
THE SETUP

1. A crowd of over 2,000 gathered along the shore.

2. A local sheriff escorted Minerva to the center of the bridge.

3. Minerva wore a flowing dress with a delicate ruffled collar, stockings, and fashionable shoes with small bows on top. She waved to the crowd.

4. A local sheriff strapped Minerva into a straitjacket.

5. Two policemen checked the jacket to confirm that it had been secured.

THE BRIDGE JUMP ESCAPE

THE REVEAL

1. Two brawny local officials lifted Minerva onto the bridge railing.
2. After a long pause, she jumped from the bridge into the icy river!
3. Seconds passed like hours. No movement. No sign of Minerva.
4. Suddenly Minerva's hand emerged from the surface of the water, waving the straitjacket in the air.
5. A local official helped Minerva onto a small boat and rowed her to shore.

The crowd that had lined up along the shore cheered the drenched and victorious Minerva, who was immediately whisked away. Later that evening she reemerged to perform at the local theater. Her stage act consisted of a series of escapes from wrist manacles, leg irons, chains, and ropes. For some performances, she might have even escaped from a linen sheet she had been sewn inside!

Minerva also staged jail escapes as part of her act. Everywhere Minerva performed, the newspapers wrote about the wonder and amazement brought about by her daring and dangerous feats. There was excitement surrounding this fearless female escape artist who took on the world of magic in remarkable ways. She challenged how women were viewed and perceived. She was far from the image of a demure and proper lady in the early 1900s.

Throughout 1908, Minerva played to packed houses across the country from Pennsylvania and Virginia to Oregon and Washington. Since William was no longer Minerva's manager, she needed to book and handle all her engagements. While performing in Maryland at an amusement park, Minerva became embroiled in a contract dispute with the manager of the venue. The theater manager insisted that she perform a Bridge Jump to draw in a crowd before each stage show. She agreed but claimed that he had insulted her during their negotiation and demanded an apology. The manager fired her on the spot. Minerva needed the income, so she ignored him and showed up every night that week to fulfill her contract. Each night, she was turned away. She refused to back down and finally sued him for the money owed for the booking and won! Minerva was not only brazen in her escapes but also in business.

By 1908, Minerva had achieved her goal of becoming a star magician. To heighten the danger of her performances, she added an even more spectacular stunt that defined and distinguished her as a woman escape artist like no other. An advertisement for Minerva's latest sensation read, "To fail in this trick means a drowning death. This is performed in full view of the audience. How long can a human being live under water without breathing?"

PRESENTING
THE
DEATH-DEFYING
WATER ESCAPE

THE SETUP

1. A large wooden barrel was filled to the brim with water.
2. Minerva arrived in a cab to the center of the bridge.
3. As many as 10,000 spectators were there to witness the escape.
4. The local police chief cuffed Minerva's hands, then locked her ankles together with metal shackles.
5. He assisted her as she climbed into the barrel, then closed and secured the lid.

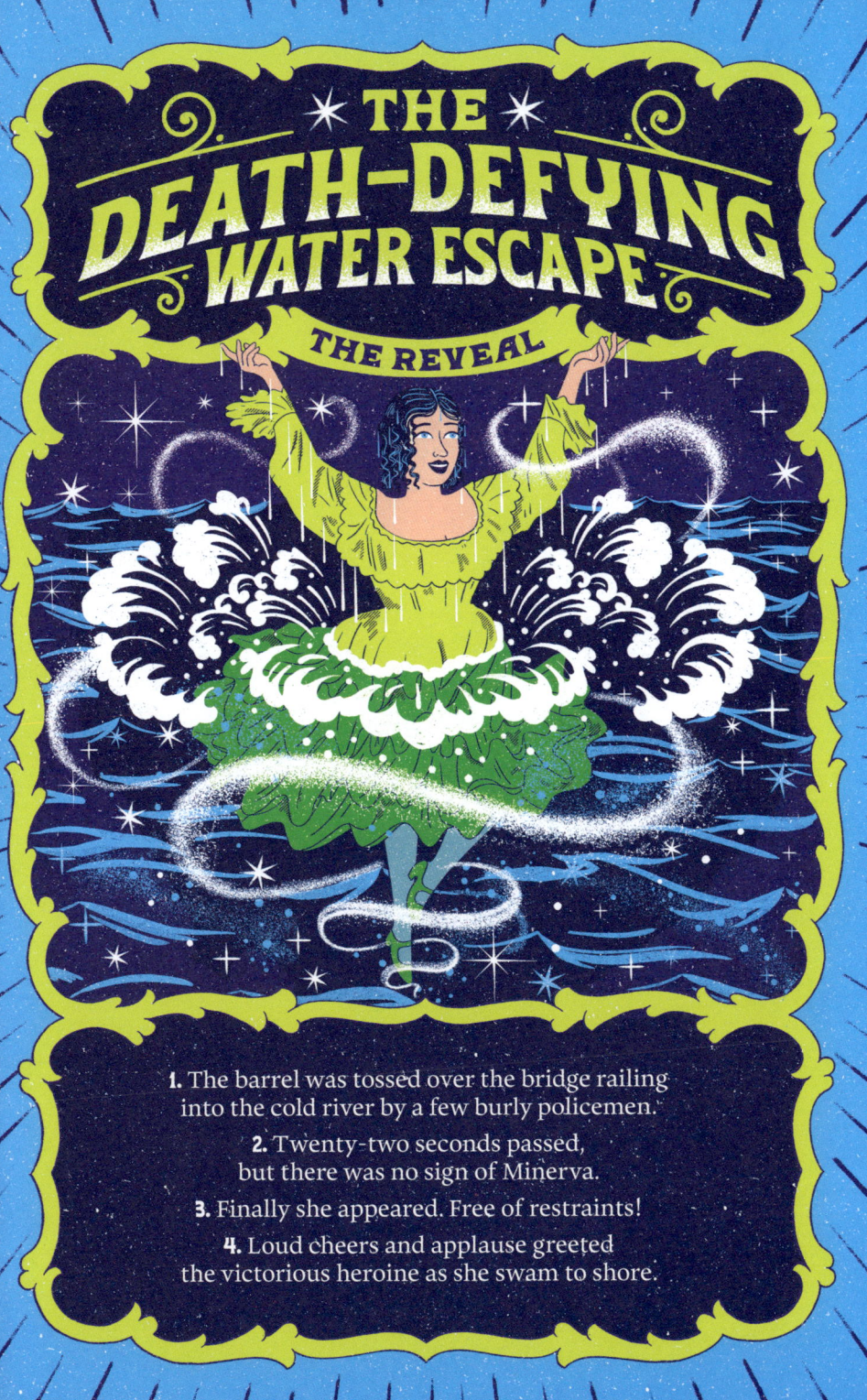

THE DEATH-DEFYING WATER ESCAPE

THE REVEAL

1. The barrel was tossed over the bridge railing into the cold river by a few burly policemen.

2. Twenty-two seconds passed, but there was no sign of Minerva.

3. Finally she appeared. Free of restraints!

4. Loud cheers and applause greeted the victorious heroine as she swam to shore.

THE HOUDINI RIVALRY

While on tour in Europe, Minerva not only took on the most dangerous feats of magic of the time, but dared to compete with the Great Harry Houdini. As the physical stakes increased, so did the drama between them. Word of mouth spread that Harry was upset with Minerva's copycat water escape. His act had involved a large milk can being submerged in a river while he was chained and handcuffed. In Harry's mind, the only difference between the two stunts was that Minerva used a water barrel instead of a milk can. Since Minerva was attracting large crowds, it's possible jealousy could have been at play. Despite the drama, Minerva ignored Houdini's public complaints and grumblings. That didn't stop the rivalry from heating up. Minerva claimed that Houdini's assistants tainted the water in her water barrel before one of her shows while on tour in England. When it came time for her to step into the barrel to perform the stunt, she felt a burning sensation. She quickly closed her eyes to avoid blindness and jumped out of the barrel to safety. The alleged attempt at sabotage was never proven. Minerva may have invented the incident for publicity, but she stuck to her story!

ESCAPING THE SHACKLES OF MARRIAGE

Minerva's hard work and drive led to more bookings in England, France, and Hungary. The Queen of Mystery returned to her home country of Germany, this time as a star. With each engagement, she garnered rave reviews. When Minerva sailed back to America eighteen months later, she joined yet another tour across the country, performing in neighboring Canada and in Cuba. Minerva had perfected her escape skills and earned a reputation as a top attraction not to be missed.

While her life as a solo woman magician was thriving, her marriage to William had come to an end. Minerva filed for divorce on November 19, 1909, in Chicago. One journalist noted that this might have been Minerva's first matrimonial escape, but it wouldn't be her last! Minerva insisted that she would never take another chance at love or marriage again. "Once was enough," she declared.

But a year later, she married her new manager, Charles M. J. Haugeros. After that short-lived marriage, Minerva met renowned magic inventor, illusion-maker, and magician Guy Garrett. They shared their passion for magic but never performed together. They were married in 1911, and she divorced him in 1919, claiming abandonment. While married to Guy, Minerva began to step away from performing. After divorcing him, she married two more times: first to James Backus in 1930 until his passing in 1941, and then to Louis Brisbane in 1955.

OUT OF THE SPOTLIGHT

Although still only in her thirties, the physical and emotional toll of Minerva's high dives and barrel escapes had weighed on her. The rigorous touring schedule and travel had left her depleted. She had grown weary of pushing her body to its limits with her high-flying escapes. By the time she turned thirty-five, she stopped performing altogether and retreated to private life.

During Minerva's career, she claimed to have escaped from over a hundred locked jail cells, sixty-three of them in America. Just as Dixie Haygood (Annie Abbott) had portrayed women as stronger than men, Minerva had shown the world that women could perform high-stakes escapes just as well as men. She challenged the conventions of the time, when women were expected to stay at home in the shadows. Minerva lived an unconventional life, marrying multiple times, and never settling down or having children. She thrilled audiences with her unique skills and irrepressible courage, relying on her physical strength and clever illusions to take on the impossible. She escaped chains, shackles, and even death in front of thousands of spectators.

On March 27, 1955, at seventy-seven, Minerva quietly passed away. She was laid to rest next to her fourth husband, James Backus, in Santa Clara, California. The spot reserved for her on the gravestone has no name engraved on it. Minerva's life and legacy as an extraordinary woman magician simply vanished.

MINERVA,
Handcuff Queen at Luna Park.

C.M.J.
HAUGEROS
MINERVA
121 WEST 42 ST.
NEW YORK
CITY·N·Y
U.S.A

American Queen of Mystery

MINERVA

Originator of the Death Def
Water Escape.

Failure in this Sensational
means a Drowning Deat

LUNA PARK

ADVANCED VAUDEVILLE.
AFTERNOON—EVERY WEEK-DAY—EVENING.
MINERVA

HANDCUFF QUEEN—More Wonderful Than
HOUDINI.
5—OTHER STAR ACTS—5
5,000 SEATS FREE.

**Special
Notice**
au10-6t.18

Minerva will jump from the
long Highway bridge, strapped
in a straight jacket, Wednes-
day, August 12, at 5 p.m.

MINERVA, QUEEN OF HANDCUFFS

MINERVA

THEY COULDN'T DROWN

ELLEN EMMA ARMSTRONG

MISTRESS OF MODERN MAGIC

THE ARTIST

DECEMBER 7, 1905 – MARCH 21, 1994

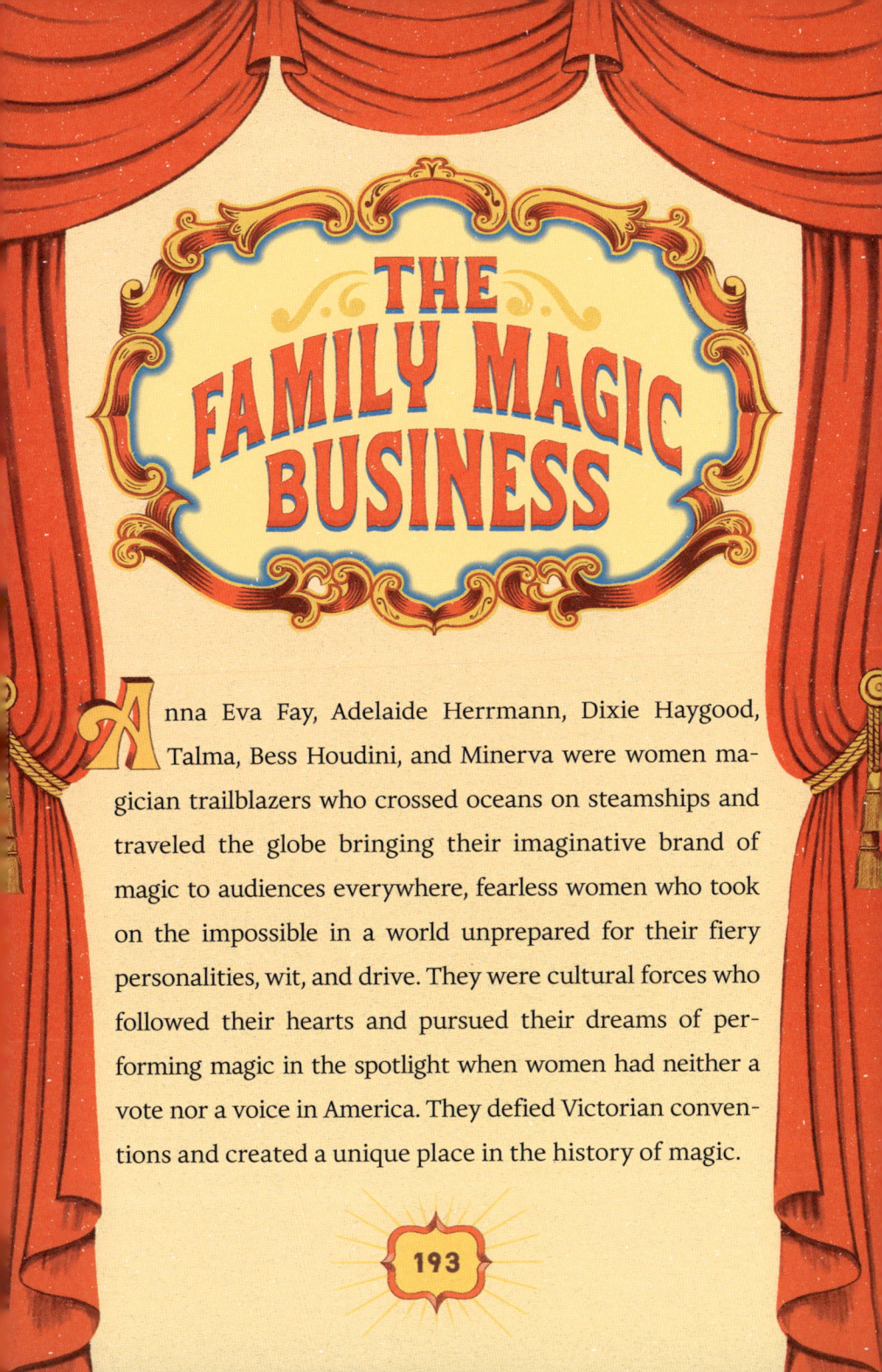

THE FAMILY MAGIC BUSINESS

Anna Eva Fay, Adelaide Herrmann, Dixie Haygood, Talma, Bess Houdini, and Minerva were women magician trailblazers who crossed oceans on steamships and traveled the globe bringing their imaginative brand of magic to audiences everywhere, fearless women who took on the impossible in a world unprepared for their fiery personalities, wit, and drive. They were cultural forces who followed their hearts and pursued their dreams of performing magic in the spotlight when women had neither a vote nor a voice in America. They defied Victorian conventions and created a unique place in the history of magic.

Ellen Emma Armstrong stands among these extraordinary conjurors as America's first African American woman magician to ever headline a magic show. She was born on December 7, 1905, in Spartanburg, South Carolina. Her life began during a time of struggle and adversity for Black Americans. After slavery was declared illegal, cruel new legislation emerged in the form of Jim Crow laws. These unjust laws, passed by local and state legislators mostly in the American South, prevented African Americans from entering public theaters, parks, schools, and restaurants. Hotels, bathrooms, building entrances, and elevators had clearly designated areas marked "whites only." Resistance could result in violence and personal harm. Yet, during this time of fear and intimidation, Ellen more than survived. She spun her difficult beginnings into a bold and daring life of entertainment. A Black woman performing as a solo magic act just didn't exist until Ellen stepped onstage.

From the beginning, it seemed like the odds were against Ellen. Her mother, Mabelle White, died when she was just a newborn. John Hartford Armstrong was left to raise his daughter on his own. Ellen's grandparents cared for her while John traveled for work. John, the son of a white slaveowner and Black enslaved mother, worked as a professional magician. He performed stage illusions with his brother Thomas in an act called the

Armstrong Brothers. A third brother, Leonard, worked behind the scenes arranging the bookings, sponsors, and props. During the late nineteenth century, magic secrets were passed down from one magician to the next behind closed doors, so it would have been extremely difficult for a Black man in the segregated South to gain access to this mysterious, mystical art. John Armstrong found a way to break through. In 1888, when he was fifteen years old, a traveling French magician performed at the Augusta Exposition in his home state of Georgia. John became intrigued by the conjuror and the tricks he performed. He had never seen anything like it. He watched in awe as magic uplifted the crowd. Inspired, he snuck backstage and volunteered to assist the magician in exchange for magic lessons. The magician agreed!

John practiced what he learned and trained until he began a career as a professional magician. His innate talent and natural charisma led to engagements all along the East Coast on the Black Lyceum and Chautauqua circuits. The venues were designated for African American entertainers. John distinguished himself from the minstrel shows that featured white actors in blackface and depicted African Americans negatively. He also distanced himself from medicine shows, where magic acts were used to draw in an audience, with the real goal of promoting and selling miracle cures for whatever ailed them. It was important for John to create his own style of magic and to present himself as a refined professional magician. He wore formal clothes: a collared shirt, top hat, and tails. He never learned to drive, so he hired a chauffeur to take him to all his engagements. This further added to his image as a legitimate upper-class performer.

John publicized himself as Professor J. Hartford Armstrong to send the message that his act was more than magic—it was educational. He believed that performing magic to mostly Black audiences was an opportunity to educate the crowd by showing that magic is a science, not a form of witchcraft. He played exclusively to Black audiences at the start of his career, but as his popularity grew, he sometimes performed for mixed audiences. He understood the power of his image as a Black man and wanted to bring dignity to his people through his appearance and the kind of magic he performed. He advertised his magic as clean, clever, and classy, and associated with the most popular magicians of the time, including Adelaide and Alexander Herrmann and Harry Kellar. John broke color barriers with his act by booking international engagements in Central and South American and even Cuba. He was accepted among his magician peers, but as a Black magician, he still faced challenges on the road. Hotels wouldn't accept him and his troupe while on tour, and his bookings were mostly confined to Black audiences in segregated venues, schools, community centers, public buildings, and churches.

In 1908, John married a local schoolteacher named Lillie Belle Mills. Lillie adopted young Ellen as her own. Following the marriage, the Armstrong Brothers broke up their act after fourteen years together. John began to train his young bride as a mentalist for a newly designed magic show that would feature both of them. While John performed sleight of hand and larger illusions, Lillie learned to perform the mysterious art of mind reading. She advertised herself as Lillie Belle, the World Acclaimed Mind Reader!

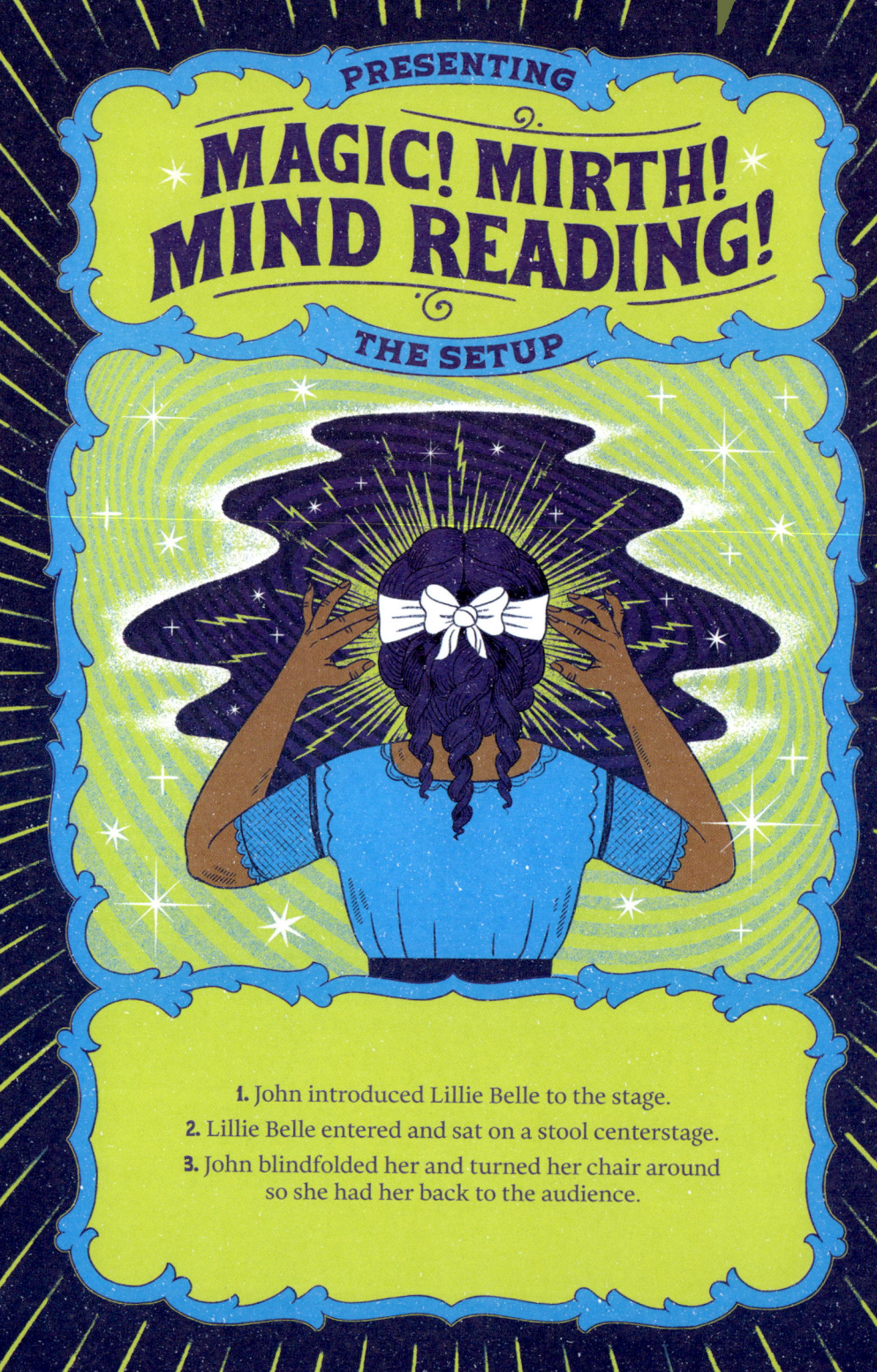

PRESENTING

MAGIC! MIRTH! MIND READING!

THE SETUP

1. John introduced Lillie Belle to the stage.
2. Lillie Belle entered and sat on a stool centerstage.
3. John blindfolded her and turned her chair around so she had her back to the audience.

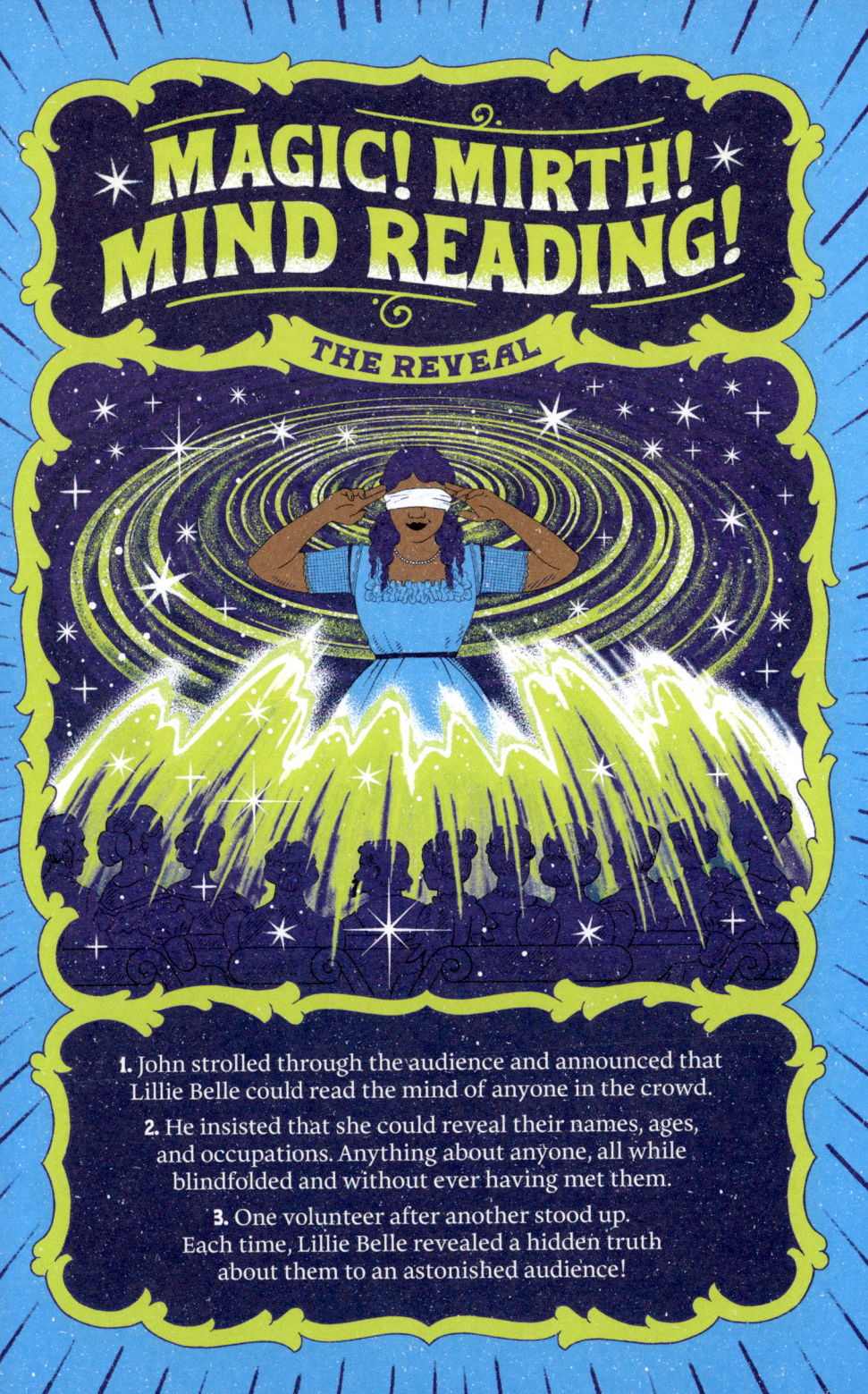

MAGIC! MIRTH! MIND READING!

THE REVEAL

1. John strolled through the audience and announced that Lillie Belle could read the mind of anyone in the crowd.

2. He insisted that she could reveal their names, ages, and occupations. Anything about anyone, all while blindfolded and without ever having met them.

3. One volunteer after another stood up. Each time, Lillie Belle revealed a hidden truth about them to an astonished audience!

John's clever illusions were performed with grace and charm. Audiences enjoyed watching him change water into wine and transform eggs into baby chicks. With a flourish and a gentle wave of his hands, he made flowers and live doves appear onstage out of thin air. To top off the show, John served endless cups of drinks to audience members from a single bowl that inexplicably never emptied. For one of his most popular signature tricks, he broke an egg into a hat, placed paper inside of it, set it on fire, and produced a full-grown chicken! John's sense of humor and clever wit combined with his exceptional magic skills set him apart. Soon his act transformed again.

THE CELEBRATED ARMSTRONGS

When Ellen turned six, she joined her father's act. She first performed a clever mind-reading trick between illusions. While John and Lillie Belle prepared their next illusion onstage, Ellen strolled through the audience. She placed her finger on a random audience member's forehead and proceeded to announce exactly what that audience member truly thought of the person sitting in the next seat. Youthful, playful, spunky. All in good fun, Ellen created the illusion of actually reading minds! She proved irresistible to the crowd and became the talk of the show. Ellen discovered immediately that she loved the stage! She also discovered something else. She could make people laugh, and she liked the way that felt.

Ellen's father was her whole world. He taught her everything he knew about magic—the sleight of hand tricks he performed, and the way in which he captured an audience's imagination. He insisted that she never talk down to an audience, but instead uplift them through magic. Every evening after the Armstrong family performed, audience members approached Ellen for autographs. She always stayed humble under her father's watchful eye. John also believed in bettering himself, the act, and especially his young daughter. He reminded her to be grateful for the family's blessed lifestyle. The Armstrongs continually evolved their tricks. They built their own sets and perfected their illusions to expand their act and stay on top of magic trends. The family act's popularity spread among African American circles in the South and throughout the East Coast. John boasted that "the Celebrated Armstrongs covered America like the sun."

Ellen had grown up on the stage. Even though she had become a key part of the show, John encouraged her to pursue a college degree when she came of age. As a young woman who was raised as an entertainer in a family show, it must have been a difficult decision for Ellen to leave her father and Lillie Belle to attend school. It was a milestone for her when she graduated Barber-Scotia College for Black women in Concord, North Carolina. After graduation, Ellen couldn't think of pursuing any life other than one filled with magic. To her father's delight, she rejoined the Celebrated Armstrongs for their next tour!

With Ellen back in the show, the Armstrongs built new momentum. Their advertisements promised the "Latest and Most Mystifying Novelties. Happy Hearts and Laughing. $5,000 invested in apparatus and paraphernalia. First, finest and foremost in their line. Endorsed by Press, Pulpit and Public. One Big Night of Music, Mirth, and Mystery. If laughing hurts you, stay at home. They will tickle your shoestrings and make your big toe laugh!"

Ellen, now in her twenties, took on greater responsibility in the act. She returned from college even more dedicated to her father's mission of spreading magic and entertainment to her community. By 1939, John had been performing as a magician for almost fifty years. His distinguished career, first with his brothers, then with Belle and Ellen, was more incredible since he had overcome the injustices facing Black entertainers in early twentieth century America. He publicized the show as "Going Fine Since 1889," referring to the first year he performed magic when he was just a teenager.

On June 16, 1939, John died unexpectedly of heart failure after a short illness. Ellen's world turned upside down. Her father had raised her to be strong in the face of adversity, but she found the pain of his loss difficult to overcome. She knew he would have wanted her to stay strong and carry on with the act. She stepped away from the stage to take time to reflect on his influence over her since she was a child, how he had mentored her, sharing all he knew about tricks and illusions. Ellen watched him bring good clean fun and high-quality entertainment to the Black community with every performance. She was indebted to him for providing her with a comfortable life despite the adversity. He showed her how to live a rich and fulfilling life by following his passion for performing magic.

After a time of mourning and reflection, there was no doubt that Ellen would carry on the Armstrong family legacy. She set aside any fear of failing to live up to her father's reputation and turned her focus to developing her own show. Her calling to use magic to elevate and educate propelled her, and soon she emerged as the first Black woman headlining magician in America!

AN ARTIST ARRIVES

(1939)

Now that Ellen had inherited her father's magic show, it meant training and perfecting the illusions and managing all the bookings. Even though time had passed since her father had first launched his act, the bigoted Jim Crow laws were still in effect in the Southern states where Ellen performed. She faced the same challenging conditions that her father had endured: performances limited to Black-only venues, separate and less desirable seating on public transportation, restricted access to restaurants and hotels while on tour. Driven by her passion for magic and her commitment to honoring the family legacy, Ellen persevered. She took on John's role as the featured act with defiance and grace. Lillie Belle traveled with Ellen and continued performing with her, playing piano and joining her in the mind-reading portion of the show. Some of the sleight of hand tricks, including the classic Miser's Dream, in which Ellen produced coins out of thin air or from behind an unsuspecting audience member's ear, were second nature to her. Other tricks in the repertoire de-

manded more practice. A particularly beautiful illusion that Ellen featured in her debut act was called the **Puzzling Parasol**. A parasol is an umbrella that protects from the sun. The illusion required a certain technique and dexterity that Ellen rehearsed until, at last, she was ready to perform it.

PRESENTING

PUZZLING PARASOL

THE SETUP

1. Lillie Belle began playing the piano.

2. Ellen entered twirling a colorful parasol, gracefully moving about the stage.

3. Ellen closed the parasol, set it aside, and covered it.

4. She produced a set of colorful scarves along with a small empty bag.

5. She placed each scarf, one by one, inside the bag.

PUZZLING PARASOL

THE REVEAL

1. With a wave of her hand, Ellen reached back inside the bag.

2. The silk scarves had inexplicably disappeared and instead she revealed the parasol cover.

3. She turned back to where she had set aside the parasol and opened it to reveal that only the bare metal frame was left!

Ellen was ready to take the helm and represent the Armstrong name. She brought elegance, beauty, and, most of all, humor to the act. She promised her audiences 250 laughs in fifty minutes! She launched her first tour with Lillie Belle in the same all-Black circuits where the Celebrated Armstrongs had once performed. They found instant success, wowing their audiences.

While Ellen continued to build her act, she gravitated toward tricks that highlighted her strengths. As a teenager Ellen had perfected a trick called **Chalk Talk**. It soon defined her particular brand of magic and showcased her artistic talents and gift for storytelling.

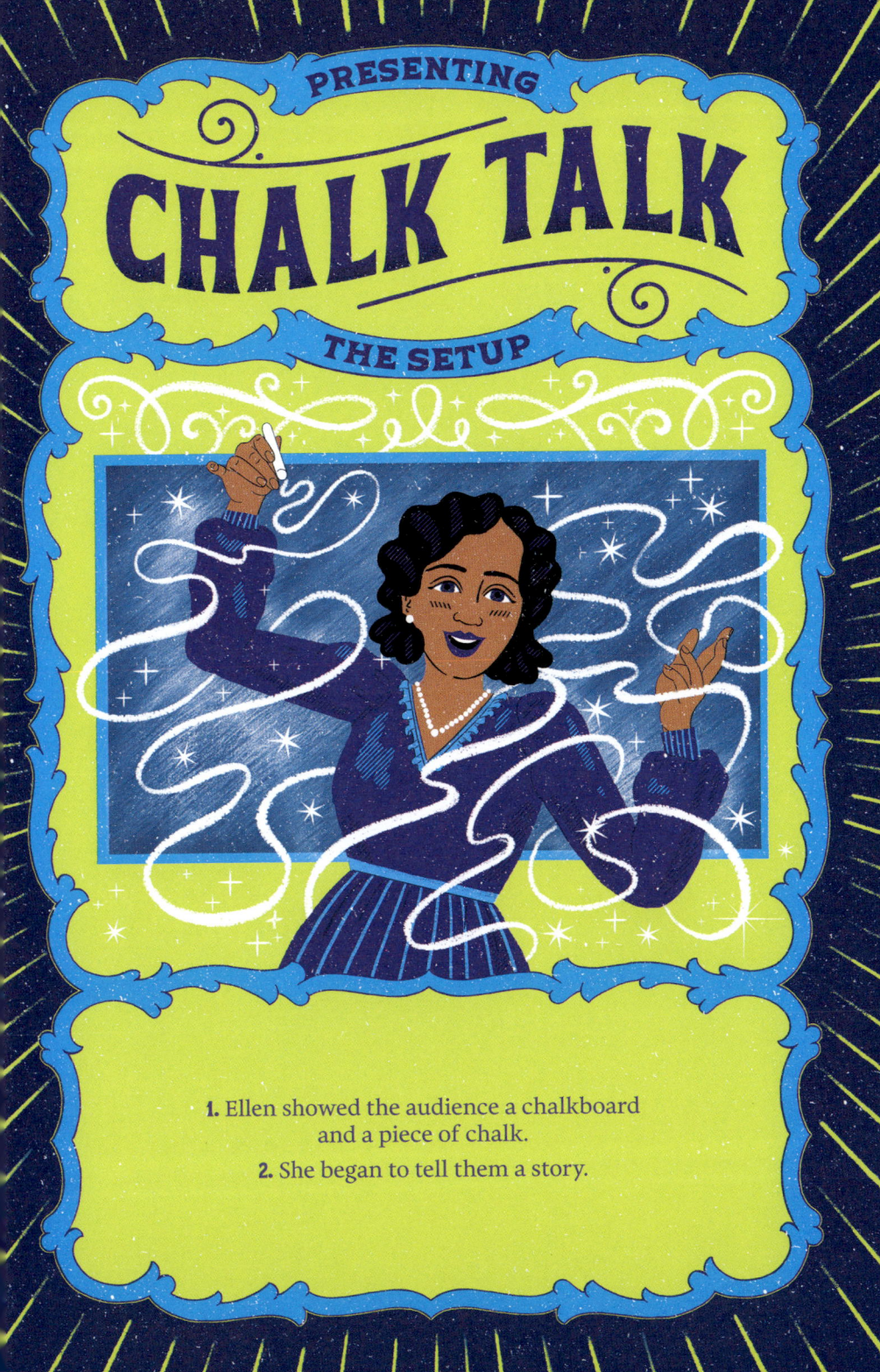

PRESENTING

CHALK TALK

THE SETUP

1. Ellen showed the audience a chalkboard and a piece of chalk.

2. She began to tell them a story.

CHALK TALK

THE REVEAL

1. Within seconds, Ellen created a doodle of the lead characters of the story as it unfolded.

2. During the storytelling, she added a doodle of a hat. Then, in a single line, she created the image of a rabbit coming out of that same hat!

3. For the finish, Ellen turned the image upside down to reveal a portrait of President Abraham Lincoln, formed by the single line doodle she drew for the story!

As Ellen varied her act over the years, she performed a version of this same trick using crayons. She would tear out the page of her sketchbook and hand the final image to an audience member as a souvenir. She billed herself as Cartoonist Extraordinary!

Ellen's success led to more travel, and she met a range of African American leaders from the church and local politics. Inspired by their commitment to raise up her community, she carried on her father's mission of educating Black audiences. John had used his magic act as a platform to enlighten, educate, and empower. Ellen continued that undertaking by building more educational messages into her storytelling and featuring important Black figures, highlighting their positive and influential roles in American culture.

One visual trick called the **Sand Frame Illusion** featured the story of Frederick Douglass, famed abolitionist and political leader, who had escaped slavery.

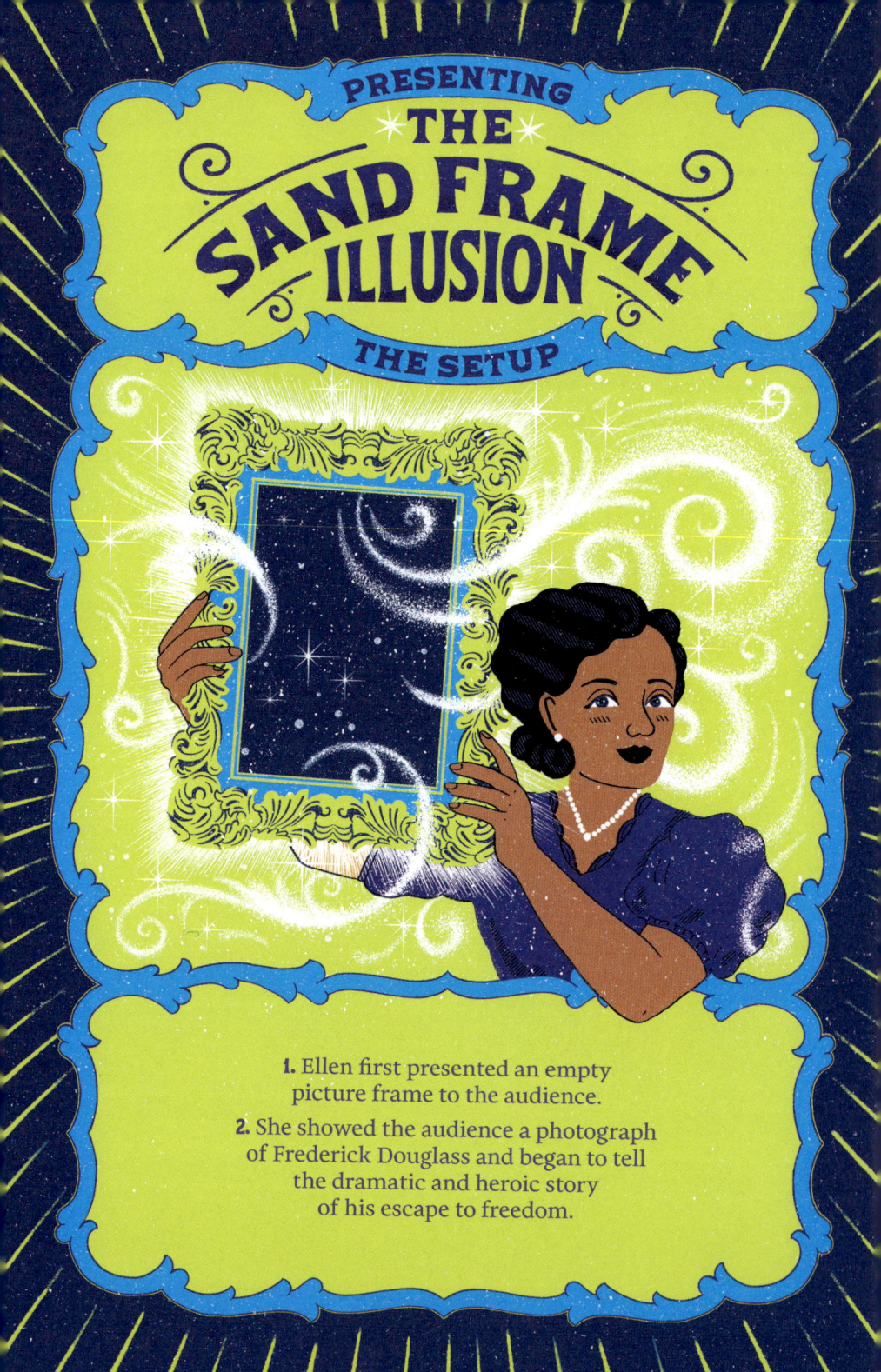

PRESENTING
THE
SAND FRAME
ILLUSION
THE SETUP

1. Ellen first presented an empty picture frame to the audience.

2. She showed the audience a photograph of Frederick Douglass and began to tell the dramatic and heroic story of his escape to freedom.

THE
SAND FRAME
ILLUSION
THE REVEAL

1. Suddenly the photo disappeared.

2. Magically, it then reappeared in the empty picture frame.

3. The audience was amazed!

4. The effect was not only entertaining but highlighted Frederick Douglass's own story of disappearing under the cover of darkness to escape slavery, and then reappearing to become an influential African American hero.

Since a big part of Ellen's mission as a magician was to educate, she later added another Black cultural icon of empowerment, contemporary hero and champion boxer Joe Louis, to her repertoire. This fearless athlete had become a source of great pride for the African American community and a hero for all of America.

In the early 1940s, Ellen found love and married a minister named Pierce Bowling. Pierce hailed from her hometown of Spartanburg, South Carolina. But married life didn't slow Ellen down. A born performer, she continued booking her act at churches, schools, and Black entertainment venues. Although Ellen never had children, she enjoyed performing for young people and customized her shows for them. It brought her great joy to entertain and educate a new generation. She kept her father's legacy alive by using magic to uplift and inspire.

THE SCRAPBOOK

While other leading women magicians such as Anna Eva Fay, Adelaide Herrmann, and Talma enjoyed press coverage in widely circulated newspapers to promote themselves, Ellen's shows were not largely reviewed in newspapers. Since her performances reached only Black audiences, she had to rely on self-promotion to get the word out about her act. Her family's reputation as high-quality entertainers landed her initial bookings, but her livelihood depended on each performance. Women, especially women of color, had to continually prove themselves. Ellen did this with a scrapbook she kept tucked in her suitcase. Just as her father had done, she saved records of her performances—tickets and playbills—as proof of the popularity and wholesome content of her shows. Glued into its pages were also letters of recommendation from her sponsors, alongside letters of praise from civic leaders and theater owners. The scrapbook was her lifeline.

Since little was documented about Ellen, these precious fragments from her past held crucial evidence about her personality, act, and career achievements that would otherwise have gone unrecorded. Sadly, many of the scrapbooks have disappeared. What remains are notes of praise from school principals, small-town preachers, and local business owners encouraging the public to attend Ellen's performances. These pieces of evidence reveal clues about her extraordinary life and career. Without these faded images, posters, and notices, Ellen's journey as a woman conjuror would still be hidden in the shadows.

THE GROUNDBREAKER

Ellen and her family performed magic for over seventy years. In 1949, she was recognized by *Ebony* magazine for her contribution to the magic world, but there are very few other records highlighting her contribution to American entertainment. Her quiet courage and determination led to a groundbreaking career. She was an original, a woman conjuror who brought dignity and humor to her performances, always shining a light

on the transformative power of magic. Her pure approach to her life and to those around her carried into her performances and was the secret ingredient to her popularity. Although a charismatic and high-energy performer onstage, privately, she lived a quiet life with friends and family. She was devoted to her small town of Spartanburg, where she lived for over fifty years.

Ellen performed for three decades as a Black woman magician headliner when there was no precedent. She was the first! Yet she never boasted about her remarkable accomplishments. On March 21, 1994, she passed away peacefully in a nursing home in Columbia, South Carolina. No one could have predicted or believed the story of a curious and gifted young Black girl in the Jim Crow South who followed her heart and created magic out of thin air until Ellen Armstrong, the Mistress of Modern Magic, stepped onstage and lived it.

COMING

ELLEN E.
ARMSTRONG
Since 1889 America's Favorite Magical Act

Presenting Magic as Formerly Done by the Original
J. HARTFORD ARMSTRONG

MING...!

ELLEN E.
ARMSTRONG

EPILOGUE

I've spent so much time getting to know the women magicians in *Vanished* that I can't get them out of my head. I've tried. The truth is that I'm going to miss them. I also keep wondering if I got it right. With nonfiction, there are leaps of faith when evidence is scarce, which was the case for these women who had been virtually forgotten from history. Weaving together their stories from fragments of images, advertisements, and other ephemera challenged me to connect the missing parts of their stories. I didn't want to disappoint them. I hope in these pages that I've shared their stories in the way they would have wanted them to be told.

I wonder now too if their stories really ended. I have a feeling there's more than meets the eye. The women conjurers in *Vanished* broke ground and paved the way for other women to carry the torch. Whether they realized it or not, they set the standard. There were innovators, rebels, and pioneers. Other women then stepped in and brought their unique magic to the stage. There was Geraldine Larsen, the first woman to perform magic on television in 1939 as the Magic Lady and Boko, who had a long career as a puppeteer and magician. Her sons, Milt and Bill, kept her magic influence alive by founding the world-famous Magic Castle in Hollywood, the internationally acclaimed private clubhouse for magicians that celebrates the magical arts seven days a week. And Dell O'Dell, the first woman to own and run a traveling circus and who starred in her television show, *The Dell O'Dell Show*. She brought glamour, style, and wit to her personal brand of magic. And Frances Willard, the daughter of famed magician Harry Willard, "Willard the Wizard," who traveled town to town as a young girl, performing in a tent show with her family of magicians. Frances went on to resurrect Anna Eva Fay's iconic Spirit Cabinet act, an influential piece of magic history, which became the centerpiece illusion of her internationally acclaimed career. These are just

a few of the incredible women who created magic from sheer will, talent, and determination—the torch carriers.

The magicians portrayed in *Vanished* opened my eyes to the adventure that comes with living out a dream, even if that dream means overcoming hardship and adversity. I understood their struggles and saw the reward of conjuring moments of wonder that inspired and lifted their audiences. I'm going to miss my new friends, but I find comfort when I watch magic now because really I'm seeing Anna's piercing and bewitching blue eyes, Adelaide's showbiz bravado and sparkle, Dixie's dangerous charm and deception, Talma's delicate beauty and skill, Bess's fiery spirit and perseverance, Minerva's strong will and bravery, and Ellen's sly smile and artistry. I see their influence, and I feel their magic.

ACKNOWLEDGMENTS

Vanished could not have appeared on these pages if it hadn't been for Dan Lazar at Writers House, who stood by this project from the beginning and believed in the idea, and in me. Dan, you are my champion, and I am forever grateful to you.

Tom Russell, who took the manuscript under his wing and helped shine a light on these hidden stories. What a joyful experience collaborating with you and bringing *Vanished* to life!

Mary Kate McDevitt, for your vibrant and colorful artistic touch.

Victoria Doherty-Munro, for your caring and keen eye throughout the journey.

Catherine Frank, who set me in the right direction from the start.

The Bright Matter team: Eugenia Lo, Jen Valero, Alison Kolani, Maddy Stone, and Rebecca Vitkus.

Brett Wright, who helped guide the first steps and who brought such careful thought and enthusiasm to the project.

Thank you to David Copperfield, Glenda Wellendorf, and Chris Kenner for inviting me inside the International Museum and Library of the Conjuring Arts and entrusting me with your priceless treasures, and for your generosity in allowing me to include my discoveries from your secret vault in *Vanished.*

To the researchers, librarians, and archivists who gave their time and excavating skills to help me uncover valuable clues about these remarkable magicians. Heather McNabb and Anne-Frédérique Beaulieu, the McCord Stewart Museum; Eric Colleary and Elon Long, the Harry Ransom Center, University of Texas at Austin; Annemarie van Roessel, the Billy Rose Theatre Division of the New York Public Library for the Performing Arts; and magician, author, publisher, and collector Mike Caveney and the Egyptian Hall Museum. Thanks to Nicole Molyneux for leading me to the Armstrong family images provided by the South Caroliniana Library, University of South Carolina, and to the Michael Claxton Collection. Also, the search tools

Ask Alexander, Conjuring Arts Research Center; Chronicling America, Library of Congress Newspaper Directory; and the International Association for the Preservation of Spiritualist and Occult Periodicals were invaluable for my research.

Magicians Michael Weber and Romany and all magicians who dare to conjure the impossible. Thanks for keeping the art alive.

To my family, and to Clare, Terri, Marco, April, Eileen, Roxanne, Brooks, Jennifer, Cylin, and Cecil. I'm grateful for all your support during the book's long journey.

Buzz, Ben, Will, and Willow. You guys are my everything! Thanks for giving me the space, time, and love to create *Vanished*!

BIBLIOGRAPHY

Copperfield, David, Richard Wiseman, and David Britland. *David Copperfield's History of Magic.* Simon and Schuster, 2021.

Harrington, Susan J., and Hugh T. Harrington. *Annie Abbott "The Little Georgia Magnet" and the True Story of Dixie Haygood.* CreateSpace Independent Publishing, 2010.

Haskins, Jim, and Kathleen Benson. *Conjure Times: Black Magicians in America.* Walker and Company, 2001.

Houdini, Harry. *A Magician Among the Spirits.* Harper and Brothers, 1924.

Hurst, Lulu. *Lulu Hurst (The Georgia Wonder) Writes Her Autobiography and for the First Time Explains and Demonstrates the Great Secret of Her Marvelous Power.* Lulu Hurst Book Company, 1897.

Jarrett, Guy E., and Steinmeyer, Jim. *The Complete Jarrett.* Hahne Publications, 2001.

229

Kalush, William, and Larry Sloman. *The Secret Life of Houdini: The Making of America's First Superhero.* Atria Books, 2006.

Kellock, Harold. *Houdini: His Life-Story.* Harcourt, Brace and Company, 1924.

Magus, Jim, and Melania Magus. *That Old Black Magic: The Lives and Legends of Great African American Magicians.* Self-published, 2020.

Steele, Margaret. *Adelaide Herrmann, Queen of Magic: Memoirs, Published Writing, and Collected Ephemera.* Bramble Books, 2012.

Wiley, Barry H. *The Georgia Wonder: Lulu Hurst and the Secret That Shook America.* Hermetic Press, 2004.

Wiley, Barry H. *The Indescribable Phenomenon: The Life and Mysteries of Anna Eva Fay.* Hermetic Press, 2005.

PHOTOGRAPH CREDITS

Billy Rose Theatre Division of the New York Public Library for the Performing Arts: pp. 74, 76 (bottom), 77 (1st, 2nd, 3rd from top), 109, 112 (bottom), 113 (top, bottom), 168 (3rd from top), 169 (bottom)

Chronicling America, Library of Congress: pp. 77 (bottom), 112 (middle), 113 (2nd, 3rd from top), 138 (top), 169 (2nd from top), 190 (2nd, 4th from top), 191 (all)

Harry Houdini Collection, Harry Ransom Center, The University of Texas at Austin: p. 164

Hays Collection: pp. 39 (2nd from top), 219 (3rd from top)

The International Museum and Library of the Conjuring Arts: pp. 50, 56–57, 59, 64, 88, 100, 137, 138 (bottom)

Magic Collection, Harry Ransom Center, The University of Texas at Austin: pp. 176–177, 190 (3rd from top)

231

McCord Stewart Museum: pp. 12, 23, 30, 34, 36, 38 (all), 39 (1st, 3rd, 4th, 5th, 6th from top), 46, 76 (1st and 2nd from top), 129, 138 (2nd, 3rd from top), 139 (all), 149, 157, 165, 166, 168 (1st, 2nd, 4th, 5th from top), 169 (1st, 3rd, 4th from top)

Michael Claxton Collection: pp. 205, 218 (all), 219 (1st, 2nd, 4th from top)

Mike Caveney's Egyptian Hall Museum: pp. 112 (top), 124, 190 (top)

South Caroliniana Library, University of South Carolina, Columbia: 195, 201, 216